Refuge from Anguish

Profugiorum ab ærumna

by Leon Battista Alberti. Architect, author, artist,
poet, priest, linguist, philosopher, and cryptographer
(1404-1472)

Content

BOOK I P01   BOOK II P46   BOOK III P77

BOOK I

Niccola, the son of Messer Veri de' Medici, a man distinguished in every aspect of character and virtue, and I, while strolling together in our grand temple, engaged in our usual manner of discussing pleasant matters related to knowledge and the exploration of worthy and rare subjects. Agnolo, son of Filippo Pandolfini, a serious and mature man of integrity, who has always been sought after and esteemed among our foremost citizens for his age and wisdom, approached and greeted us. He said, "Battista, I praise you, and I am pleased to see that, just as in other matters, you are devotedly present in this temple. It was not without reason that our wise ancestors said that the greatest effort in divine worship is made when sacred places dedicated to God are frequented. And certainly, this temple possesses grace and majesty. What I have often observed and delights me is that in this temple, I see a delightful elegance combined with robust and solid dignity, in such a way that on one hand, every part seems designed for charm, and on the other hand, I understand that everything here is constructed and intended for perpetuity. Furthermore, a temperate climate continually dwells here, one could say, like spring: outside, there may be wind, frost, and chill, but within, it is shielded from the winds, offering a mild and tranquil atmosphere. Outside, there are scorching summer heats and autumnal chills, but within, there is a very temperate refreshment. And if it is true, as they say, that pleasures are heightened when nature's requirements are added to our senses, who would hesitate to call this temple a haven of delights? Wherever you look, you see every part exposed to joy and happiness; it is always fragrant here, and what I value above all is the wondrous sweetness I perceive in these voices during the sacrifice and in what the ancients called mysteries. That is to say, all other repetitive modes and varieties of songs become tiresome, but this religious chant never ceases to delight you. Consider the genius of that musician, Timotheus, the inventor of so many things! I don't know how it affects others, but I can affirm this about myself: these chants and hymns of the church have the power to quiet any disturbance within me and move me to a certain indescribable tranquillity of spirit, filled with reverence towards God. And what brave heart could remain unmoved when it hears those pure and true voices ascend and descend with such tenderness and flexibility? I assure you that whenever I hear those Greek verses invoked in those mysteries and funeral ceremonies, asking for God's help in our human miseries, I cannot help but shed tears. And at times, I marvel and contemplate the great power they possess to soften our hearts. Hence, I believe the stories that say musicians were able to stir Alexander the Great to arms by singing and then to recall him to feasting. But did I do well? Perhaps I interrupted your conversation, Niccola, and went off on topics that are not suitable.

These were Agnolo's words until now. Therefore, Niccola replied to him and said: "Our discussions were not such that yours are not most suitable. And if I understand Battista's mind correctly, nothing can be more pleasing and welcome to him than hearing you and discussing learned and worthy matters. I assure you that he holds you in reverence and esteems you as much as your virtue and authority deserve. Let me tell you what I have often heard from him, that only two men seem to him to be the pride of our homeland, fathers of the senate and true moderators of the Republic: one is his own Giannozzo degli Alberti, a man of certainty as he expressed in his third book De Familia, a good and humane old man; the other is you, who can be compared to Giannozzo in every praise. You are older in the senate, foremost in authority, and unmatched in integrity. If Giannozzo had great knowledge of letters, I would say: where else could two men be found so accomplished in every virtue, or so similar in every praise? I want to infer that to Battista, who always calls you father and looks at you and listens to you with eagerness and pleasure, your discussions will be as welcome and pleasing as they are to me."

"But what shall we say? Let us leave aside the description and form of this temple. Let us not seek how much weight is imposed upon those who can support it, or how much better it could be occupied to inspire grace and admiration. That discussion can take place elsewhere. Let us come to what I desire to understand from you. Agnolo, do you believe that these exchanges and combinations of voices can uplift souls and impose various excitements and emotions upon them? It would require too much power in Battista if he could, with his musical instruments, direct the souls wherever he wished. Firstly, I am amazed by our Plato, the prince of philosophers, who affirmed that it never happened that a new mode of singing was introduced to the masses without causing some immediate public disturbance. I would not believe Plato if he persuaded me of this, nor would you praise me if I believed him. Perhaps they would say that it is an indication and sign of what they observed to have followed: but this still does not satisfy me. The true causes are different, the true indicators are those that demonstrate prepared ruins for republics, among which are immodesty, arrogance, audacity of citizens, impunity of sinning, license to mistreat the weak, conspiracies and secret meetings of those who seek more power than is suitable, obstinate wills against good advice, and similar things well known to you; they are the ones that give knowledge of the times, whether they will be prosperous or adverse. And the other, to dignify his art, said that the soul of man is composed of harmony and musical consonances. These do not satisfy me, nor do I see how the soul has any correspondence with the noise or cacophony of multiple voices and sounds. I judge that the soul is either subject or bound or subjected to these movements by something that I cannot comprehend, and not only musicians, but even philosophers with their excellent and abundant reasons cannot divert it from the cares that constantly besiege it, nor can they divert the bitterness in which our soul is inexplicably engaged. This is proven every day, as sad memories, ungrateful expectations, and harsh offenses present themselves and cling to the soul, in such a way that we must grieve and fear against our will; for no one is so foolish as not to prefer joy to sadness, hope for good rather than live in fear. And these philosophers, with their words, believe they can extinguish that which, by its very nature, can have such a profound effect on us. I don't know where this comes from, yet I feel it to be fixed and almost immortal within us mortals. Whatever it may be, it is so intense and persistent in itself, I confess, Agnolo, I do not know. But I feel it, I experience it, and it pains me. But you, as a prudent person, will determine how it should be judged. Up until now, I would agree with someone who said that such evil cannot be prevented by us except with time, by gradually weakening that force of heaven and nature; for I do not see any other way to exclude the bitterness and harshness of the soul, conceived through the injustices of fortune and the adverse events that strike us from countless directions, incessantly presenting themselves and occupying our senses and minds to the extent that we are not allowed to refute or disturb them in any way.

AGNOLO: I can clearly see that you strive to please Battista, and I'm pleased to satisfy him as well, since he delights in hearing me, and these are indeed worthy and follow-worthy discussions. I will follow your lead, Niccola, in this discourse, although I know you are not expressing your true opinion and judgment, but rather you enticed me to express mine. So, let us engage in a dialogue by recounting and gathering what someone like us would say, someone who would rather oppose the words of others through reasoning than simply assert their own. It reminds me of that debate by Xenophon, where the Median Araspas told Cyrus that men have within themselves two souls: one is a true lover of just and honourable things, while the other is the opposite, inclined toward idleness rather than industry, more devoted to pleasures than to the pursuit of worthy and rare things, driven by desire and indulgence rather than reason and steadfastness. Araspas claimed that he would abandon that sinful soul and bring along the righteous and virtuous one, with which he would serve Cyrus and fulfil his duty in warfare, wherever there was an opportunity to exercise virtue.

I confess, Niccola, that I am not entirely endowed with that virtue. I cannot claim to have completely excluded that sinful soul from myself, and sometimes I do err in that realm where they say passions, desires, pains, hopes, and similar disturbances reside. I am in an age, as you can see, having already lived for about ninety years. I have seen many things, experienced many hardships in life, and almost worn down my soul by enduring misfortunes. Yet, at times, when certain events occur, I cannot help but think of multiple things, and I find myself overwhelmed by a certain sorrow and sadness, without knowing from where or how it arises. I am overcome by indignation from numerous received injustices, irritated by the insolence of certain ambitious individuals, burdened by the audacity, recklessness, and furious impetus of those who freely trample on the righteous. And I say to myself: Agnolo, what is this to you? You

are advanced in age, and you lack none of the
desired and sought-after things of fortune. You
possess a clear and grateful spirit toward your fellow
citizens. You live, as they say, for yourself now,
and you should enjoy the present circumstances as
they are. Thus, I chastise myself with many similar
admonishments, but I achieve little for myself as
much as I desire, for the sight of things not being in
the good order I long for and strive to bring about
prevails.

However, it's not that I cannot overcome myself.
Why not? Why couldn't I do what others have done,
men who were once alive like me? How many were
there who displayed steadfastness and true courage
of spirit in difficult and harsh circumstances?
And who will forbid us, in the face of adversity
and challenges, from resisting and dispelling every
disturbance with good reason and sound judgment?
I have no doubt that if we were to strengthen
ourselves with virtue and resolutely oppose those
who offend us in a dignified manner, we would find
ourselves to be no less than men, possessing no
less power than men are capable of. And what the
times, that is, the succession and variety of events
governed by nature, impose upon us will never
surpass the abilities bestowed upon us by nature
itself. They write that Socrates was incessantly ill-
treated by his disobedient and troublesome wife, and
he was insulted in various ways by his disrespectful
children at home. Moreover, outside his home, he
was constantly harassed by many insolent ruffians
and by those comic poets who incessantly targeted

him with various insults. Despite being assailed from so many sides, he lived with an equanimous spirit and an unchanged countenance, untroubled by any disturbance of fortune or any ruin of his own affairs. Therefore, Socrates achieved this not through celestial intervention, but through his own will; he chose to endure, and by choosing, he was able to endure. Socrates is not the only one worthy of praise in this regard; many others are mentioned who possessed a similarly upright character. Among them was Diogenes the Cynic, a man debased and humiliated in his extreme poverty, often even physically assaulted. Yet, he could endure his hardships and the injustices of others as much as he desired. I could also mention Pyrrho, Heraclitus, Timon, and others, who, through self-discipline, were able to maintain their composure in the face of disturbances and withstand the storms of their own fortune. Pericles, a highly esteemed and prominent figure among the Greeks and his fellow citizens, endured an entire dinner until late at night in the company of a reckless slanderer and reviler. To further demonstrate his own worth and constancy, he allowed himself to be followed and berated all the way to his doorstep. Moreover, with an unfazed demeanour and unaltered words, he commanded his servants to provide light and companionship to this offensive and uncivilized individual wherever he wished to go. Pericles did not want to, in punishing another's wrongdoing, contaminate himself or allow the disturbance that had been brought upon him to affect him. By not receiving it, he rendered it insignificant and extinguished it, as he had determined to do by enduring and conquering himself, thereby proving himself worthy of his virtue. What do you think of that Metellus Numidicus, who was exiled by his fellow Roman citizens for no reason other than his excessive virtue? Or when he was in Asia, in the middle of a theatre performance, he was informed that his homeland was recalling him with the greatest of honours. Even in his immense joy, he displayed constancy, and no change was seen in his demeanour.

Therefore, in both prosperous and adverse circumstances, we find that human beings can control themselves in ways that many deny. I am amazed at their judgment when they believe that our desires and appetites cannot be moderated in these fleeting and fragile matters, even though they see that those who do not abandon themselves can withstand the most severe and harsh circumstances, almost beyond what nature requires. How many endure extreme torment and unbearable pain with unwavering and courageous spirits! And who doesn't know that if we moderate our desires and restrain our wills, there is nothing left to provoke any disturbance within us? Can humans endure things that are naturally bitter and most unpleasant, but not things that are easy and readily available? Mucius Scaevola placed his hand in the midst of fire, and Pompey put his finger in it; and many others, as recorded by the historian Valerius, could endure, where and as much as it did not displease them, not only slight movements of the soul but also severe pains.

But why do we recount these extremely rare individuals? And tell me, don't we see our lowly servants every day, oppressed by their circumstances, worn down by hardships, weary from toil, yet laughing and singing amidst their misfortunes? If someone were to ask them, "Why do you laugh?" I believe they would respond, "Because I like it." And why do you sing? "Because I want to sing and be at peace and rejoice in my own way." Does their fortune weigh them down? If it did, they would not be free to laugh or sing so light-heartedly. If it doesn't weigh them down, where does this come from, other than from the rational desire to endure what they must suffer out of necessity? By wanting it this way, do they make their pain less burdensome or strengthen themselves to bear it? Or perhaps, by wanting it so, they simply propel every annoyance away from themselves.

Therefore, let us not consider what is within our power to do as so grave or bitter, but rather as something we can make smaller and less difficult. It is like the example of a column: as long as it stands upright and firmly grounded, it not only supports itself but also bears the weight placed upon it. Yet, the same column, when it deviates from its upright position due to its inherent burden and weight, collapses. Similarly, our soul, as long as it conforms to the rectitude of truth and does not stray from reason, what burden imposed upon it will bring it down? If the soul leans toward some crooked opinion, it falls and loses its balance due to its own inclination. I remember seeing our youth engaging in fistfights, giving and receiving blows, bruising and breaking their faces, hands, and chests, returning weak and bruised, without uttering the slightest groan amidst such pain. Yet, on other occasions, I may have seen one of them loudly proclaim their impatience and lack of endurance from a mere scratch. And why does this happen? Is it not because in the former case, the right mindset of manliness leads them to willingly endure, and by wanting to endure, the pain becomes small and bearable, while in the latter case, the effeminate softness of the soul, twisted and inclined towards impatience and childish intolerance, takes over?

Hermes Trismegistus, the ancient writer, said: "Will, oh Asclepius, arises from counsel." Therefore, those who counsel well can achieve whatever they desire. The soul must be inclined towards virtue. Reason should guide it, and the soul will always be obedient to reason as long as its perverse will does not lead it astray. It should always be ready to seek good counsel in life, in order to find a way to be pleasing to oneself, agreeable to others, and beneficial to many.

However, one cannot judge what one is capable of before putting it to the test. And by testing oneself, even if one is not initially successful, they will become capable of overcoming any adverse insult by conquering themselves. Yet, many of us lack confidence and, like an inexperienced and timid soldier, we flee at the first noise and shadow of enemies, succumbing in our hearts before we even know the extent of our capabilities. Just as they say that many would have acquired wisdom if they had not first convinced themselves of their own wisdom, similarly, on the other hand, there are quite a few who remain without praise because they did not trust that they could do what they were actually capable of doing, even though they had the freedom to do so. Thus, it seems clear among us that when we are well-advised, we can accomplish as much as we desire and establish within ourselves in terms of our soul, will, thoughts, and emotions.

NICCOLA: Ah, Agnolo, what a harsh and unfair fate it must be for mortals if in this life we cannot find anyone so ignorant of knowledge, so devoid of reason, who, upon hearing these profound and widely accepted truths of yours, would not agree and acknowledge the truth of your words. On the other hand, there is no shortage of those who are skilled and well-practiced in the praised arts of living a good and happy life, yet fail to put into action what they affirm in words. Let us ponder this for a moment. If I were to ask the brother, father, or mother of one of those brave citizens who perished, overcome by Hannibal near Lake Trasimene, which is close to Cortona, "Why do you grieve? What good do your tears do? Do you not know that the value of these things subject to fortune depends solely on our opinion, whether good or bad? Whatever happens to us mortals should never be considered or deemed as bad, except to the extent that it harms us. Nothing harms us except to the extent that it makes us worse. Injustice, treachery, and cruelty do not make you worse, but rather the person in whom they reside.

Regardless of any adverse fortune that befalls you, regardless of any injury caused by wicked men, there will never be anyone who becomes worse except to the extent that they choose to suffer themselves, to have ill will towards themselves. Death is the natural condition for one who is born, imposed upon them from the very first day they appear in life. And for those who deeply reflect upon the miseries of our existence, death is nothing more than an escape from a most laborious prison and a constant turmoil and storm of the soul. It is beneficial for those who have shed their blood for the salvation of their homeland to depart from life with praise, merit, and grace,"
- I say, Agnolo, if you were to utter similar words in the presence of those afflicted individuals, what would they reply? I believe the mother, overcome by grief, would pay little attention and understand very little of your words. Perhaps the father, being more mature in age and wisdom, would respond, "Agnolo, what you say is true; however, what weighs heavily on me is what is continually burdensome, and where it burdens me, do not doubt that it causes me pain." The brother, perhaps, would reply, "If suffering the hardships and calamities were as easy for us as it seems to be for you, learned man, to debate about them, then rest assured that I would have removed this most ungrateful suffering from my soul. But I feel, through my own pain, that which I cannot express in words, which prevents me from agreeing with the arguments you have presented." I believe this would be their response. And perhaps if among them there was one of those severe and haughty Stoics, the inventors and debaters of these

disciplines, they would respond, saying, "Do you not remember that we persevere in every duty and steadfastness? These transient and fragile things are completely excluded from our thoughts and desires, and our souls are devoted to pursuits through which we live a blessed life and acquire immortality." Such, I believe, would be their words. But what of their actions? How would they align with their words? I envision them debating with a majestic air of words and gestures, with a severity of abstract sentences supported by some syllogism, with a grandeur of their opinions that shadows the soul, and it almost seems sacrilegious to think that they could be wrong in their assertions. Listen to their divine oracles: "Know yourself, mortal. Nature is satisfied with few and insignificant things. A wise person never lacks what is excellent, and misfortune never befalls them. They always live free and happy." Then they proudly display their ambitious austerity by reproaching those who indulge in pleasures, biting at those who care about fleeting and fragile things, persecuting those who succumb to sorrow, making enemies of those who fear danger, and hating those who don't exit life with an invincible and undisturbed spirit. They are truly remarkable individuals, rare men! And how do you, through your actions, approve of their words? What would become of you, given the opportunity, if you didn't prefer to live a lavish and splendid life rather than a poor one besieged by many hardships?

Crates, the philosopher, desired a magnificent house, royal decorations, various ornaments, gem-studded golden vases, and silver dining tables—all things he preached should not be valued. Aristippus, another philosopher, bought a partridge for fifty drachmas. Socrates, the philosopher, presented Dionysius the tyrant with a golden cup as a reward for outdrinking everyone else. Even the philosopher Lacydes became paralyzed from excessive drinking. I won't recount Bion, the philosopher, who, when asked what made him happiest in life, replied: making money. But I am amazed by our Aristotle, who bathed in warm oil for luxury and then sold it to his fellow citizens out of greed. And Zenon, the stoic, the father and advocate of this austere and dreadful philosophy, who prescribes unwavering strictness and constantly argues against fortune, rejecting all its indulgence and benefits—how does he behave in practice? He heard that his possessions had been burned and destroyed by enemies, and he became so disturbed that even King Antigonus, who esteemed him as almost a mortal god on Earth, was astonished and perhaps judged him as I do: many speak boldly of harsh and difficult things in the shadow and leisure, but I believe they would not endure them well in reality. Who was more obstinate in criticizing those who yield to fortune and do not affirm that virtue alone is the greatest good for mortals? Who was more vehement in reproaching such superstitions than our Latin stoic Seneca? And what was he like in reality? How different from his words! The historian Cornelius writes that he feared death so much that, to avoid falling into the traps he feared from Nero and his poisons, he dared only eat raw fruits and vegetables and drink water only from underground springs.

I could tell you many similar stories. But for what purpose? Only to convey what I feel and judge, and to say: If these learned and highly experienced men, inventors, defenders, and embellishers of these impressive rather than true sayings, either could not, in our view, be less concerned or perhaps, in your wise opinion, failed to properly value transient things and not fear adversity, then what hope do we lesser individuals, with less intellect, condition, and profession, have? If I'm not mistaken, we all desire to live without worry and bitterness. But what about me? What if I don't know, and not knowing, I can't? Or if I can't have everything I want? Some were able to endure pain, not care about misery, and laugh at their misfortune. And Mucius Scaevola was able to endure the burning of his hand. Many fears, angers, and similar frenzies can inflict greater cruelties upon us. Dido, driven by madness, killed herself. Many, fearing greater torments, decided to end their lives. And those others eager for glory, who proudly displayed remarkable toughness in their demeanour and words against circumstances and disturbances, God knows if their souls were calm and tranquil. And yet, if there was someone in whom his own misfortunes did not evoke human feelings and emotions, he was either a god or certainly not a human being. Whoever does not feel the things felt by countless other humans is not truly human. If charity resides in human hearts, if love has a place there, then anger, indignation, and similar emotions must also exist. So, why be surprised if a human soul desires its own well-being? It would be a miracle, or rather inhuman, not to desire it, and in desiring it, not to feel sorrow for not having it. If there is a sense of harm and enmity, who will be unaffected by their own misfortunes? We must seek good counsel with reason and align our souls with virtue. Oh, Angelo, remember the saying of the ancient Gion: "It hurts a bald man as much as a well-haired one when you pluck his hair." But why do we amuse ourselves with words when deeds are needed? Caesar said to Sallust: "Whoever gives advice must be free from every disturbance." And yet we expect that a soul struck by adverse events, fallen into misery, and tormented by pain will offer sound advice to itself. "An unsound mind," as the poet Ennius said, "always wanders."

But I don't want to digress, as I would be long-winded. I desire from these learned individuals, as from a skilled navigator and guide, not that they engage in a debate with me— for one must seek shelter from the storm and escape the onslaught of adverse winds— but that they show me the way and method to reach a place where I can find rest and tranquillity. Just as these philosophers, healers of the human mind and moderators of our souls, I wish they would teach me not to feign and disguise my outer appearance, but rather to avoid disturbances inwardly and cleanse my soul, as they claim can be done, with a certain reason and method.

AGNOLO: You see, Niccola, these are matters that should be reasoned about with more leisure and deliberate thought, rather than debated. I will remain opposed to you as I began, for I see that you are prepared to refute me, and I perceive your sharp and quick intellect. It is not hidden from me that skill of yours, by which you study to conceal that commonplace art of argumentation during debates, and it delights you. But do you believe that I am unaware that you hold the same views on these matters as all the learned do? That one who wishes to oppose fortune, withstand adverse circumstances, and care for nothing but virtue, can do so? Let us not dwell on this any longer, but let us consider this power, its nature and extent. I could not paint or sculpt Hercules, a faun, or a nymph out of wax, because I am not skilled in those crafts. Perhaps Battista here could, as he takes pleasure in and writes about such things. You, Niccola, just like me, cannot fence, throw a lance, or wrestle. Perhaps Battista here, in his robust age, who has practiced and trained in such matters, could. No, Battista could not, like that athlete Milo, carry a live ox on his shoulders, nor, like Aulus Numitorius, a centurion and comrade of the deified Julius Augustus, restrain with one hand the onslaught of several mares, nor could he be like that Atamantes whom Pliny saw parading in the theatre dressed in fifty leaden cuirasses and wearing sandals weighing five hundred pounds. Nor could Cicerone, while holding his enemy Clodius in contempt and hatred, truly praise him for his words and deeds. Thus, we understand that some things are beyond our natural capabilities, and some are not granted to us, not by nature, but by our own inertia, laziness, and conceived opinions. You said that everyone would prefer to live free and unburdened in those matters that are easier to debate than to endure. But what is difficult for these debaters does not seem possible to us. Look, Niccola, if that is the case, then where everyone can, few truly wish to merit praise for their virtue. You recounted the tales of one and another who were lavish and enamoured with transient things. Who praises in them what was not their obligation? And what are we debating, what they did, or rather what they could and should have done? And if we are to argue and determine the reasons and manner of living well and being praised based on their lives and conduct, let us recount those many others, also philosophers, who were content with a single worn-out garment, who dwelled in a wretched and decaying vessel for shelter, who lived on nothing but cabbage, who renounced all things fragile and transient to the extent that they wouldn't even keep a simple bowl for themselves. I won't recount them, as I too seek to avoid being long-winded. But you, a learned man, recall them to memory and consider why these individuals of mine were able to do what yours did not desire, and think about why your counterparts did not choose what they could have, equal to mine. You will find that these individuals were able to do so because they sought to conquer their own desires and willpower, while the others did not seek to restrain and moderate themselves, and thus, being unburdened and unrestrained, they struggled to contain themselves in their own duties. Seneca avoided falling into the traps and poison of Nero. That wise Agamemnon, as recounted by Homer, said that no one should be reproached, day or night, if they made every effort to avoid encountering harm. Avoiding inconveniences is one thing, but succumbing to defeat without first planning and testing oneself and one's virtues is another. The former is prudence, to anticipate and avoid displeasure; the latter is cowardice, to abandon oneself. And true fortitude is said to be like the palm tree, a tree that always bends and pushes against its burden.

I confess that someone who has experienced the hardships of life, the harshness of existence, and has already travelled the paths of suffering will be better able to understand this. You may ask, then, what is the cause of such disturbance in our reason and duty? I will answer with what just came to my mind, and let us consider, Niccola, if I am speaking the truth. Nature made our minds capable of eternity, simple and uncompounded, moved by nothing but themselves. I believe that eternity is nothing more than a certain perfection and unbroken continuity of life, always being one and the same. Motion, I believe, is what first joined and assigned itself to life. I won't delve into the movements of the mind here but be persuaded that the mind can never remain idle; it is always engaged in some investigation, arrangement, or apprehension of things. If these things are weighty, worthy, and capable of fulfilling the mind, nothing else can immerse it. If they are trivial, they will float amid the waves of our thoughts and, as often happens, sway from one thing to another until they strike against the rocks of harsh memories or firm wills within us, causing repeated and heavy impacts within our chests. Furthermore, our minds become disturbed when they are detached from reason and guided by opinion to judge wrongly about what is good or not, as we frequently see many infected by this common corruption of life, who weep and rejoice more to satisfy the judgment and senses of others than themselves. But let me explain in what category I place myself among mortals. If I were one of the unfortunate ones, Niccola, I would long for my cherished possessions, and I would not claim to possess such absolute and perfect virtue that the loss of my belongings would not cause me pain. Instead, I would seek ways and means to free myself from all mental distress. And as far as I can tell, it is readily available and almost within everyone's reach to find peace from every perturbation before they strike and even after they have been conceived. Now that our reasoning has led us to this point, let us together acknowledge whether I am mistaken.

Let's start from this point. The disturbances, let me put it this way, rain down and pour into our vacant minds. But from where do they come? Surely some will say they arise from the wickedness of the times, or from our own unjust fortune, or from some harsh circumstances, or from the wickedness and dishonesty of other people, or from our own errors. Otherwise, I see no reason for bitterness or discontent to arise within us. But, I will say, nothing external can affect our minds except to the extent that we allow it. Here's a fitting analogy. Just as we prepare and equip ourselves for the storms of winter, covered and protected by clothing, walls, our shelters and retreats, and if even the annoyance of snow, the discomfort of winds, the harshness of cold besiege and confine us, we resist by putting glass in the windows, carpets at the doors, and block every passage through which winter's harm can reach us. And if we are strong and resolute, we overcome its severity and bitterness, exerting and stimulating within us the innate warmth bestowed upon our bodies by nature to sustain our lives. If, on the other hand, we are frail and weak, we rely on fire, the sun, and hot springs. Similarly, we must train and prepare our minds for the volatilities, assaults, and storms of fortune. We must shut off every avenue of disturbance and ignite and cultivate that innate spark within our souls, which nature has added and infused in us for immortal eternity. We will train and prepare our minds against the upheavals of the times and the ruins of adverse events, first by self-reflection and self-awareness, then by judging and determining the nature of transitory and fragile things, not according to the error of opinion, but based on the truth and certainty of reason.

Tales, the philosopher, used to say that it is difficult to know oneself. I'm not sure how to interpret his statement, but to me, it doesn't seem difficult to know myself as a human being, similar to other people as described by Apuleius. And who doubts that reason exists in man? Listen to him speak, and you will be convinced that the soul of man is immortal. Look at his body, prone to weakness and decay; observe how his mind is light and restless, almost always filled with anxiety; acknowledge that his body often becomes a burden to him in various ways; recognize the vast differences in customs among men. You cannot deny that they share similar errors: they dare too much, persist in hopes, exhaust themselves in uncertain and useless pursuits; their transient possessions die one by one; the multitude lives on perpetually; they change from generation to generation; their age flies swiftly; slow to acquire wisdom, quick to embrace death, complaining in life, they inhabit the earth. Therefore, by reflecting and recognizing ourselves, we will arrive at these thoughts: Why was I born? Did I come into life merely to waste my empty and purposeless existence? Where did this intellect, this cognition, reason, and memory come from? Are they not infinite and immortal within me? And shall I allow myself to wither away and rot in idleness, buried amidst the lotus of delights and pleasures? Shall I not judge it my duty, by engaging in noble and worthy pursuits, to cultivate myself and deserve the rewards of my own industry and virtue? Will I not strive diligently to strip away and cleanse from myself every vice and moral decay? These two things, as Seneca the philosopher said, are given to us by God above all others: reason and society. Shall I let them be extinguished within me due to laziness and inertia, believing them to be worthless? Or perhaps I will only employ them in serving this body of mine and these tiresome and troublesome limbs? Will it not delight me to employ them for the glory and immortality of my name, fame, and dignity, for the sake of my family and my homeland? Will I not constantly remind myself that I was born not only, as Anaxagoras replied, to contemplate the heavens, the stars, and the whole universe, but also, as Lactantius affirmed, to recognize and serve God, for serving

God means nothing more than dedicating oneself to promoting goodness and upholding justice? This is what is required of me, and this is my spontaneous and willing resolve. So, let us direct our minds towards these noble and pleasing works, pleasing to our Father and Creator God. Our good actions will not befit the company of the wicked we have chosen to support, nor can we uphold justice unless we are enemies of all injustice. Therefore, let us dedicate our minds to being free of all injustice and filled with goodness. In doing so, we will be well prepared for every duty of humanity and the worship of virtue, serving the natural society and true religion, and excelling in our lives by being steadfast and free.

They say that fickleness is an enemy to tranquillity. Lysias, the orator, attributes freedom to doing nothing against one's will. No one is fickler than someone who doesn't anchor their desires to any certainty, and no one goes against their own desires as much as someone who desires what they do not have because what they do to obtain it, they would rather not do. To overcome these troublesome desires, it is beneficial to consider things with reason and truth, not with the kind of opinion that Ariston, the philosopher, criticized in us mortals, wondering why it is that men indulge in the belief that they are happier with superfluous things rather than necessary ones. It will greatly benefit us to establish that good and necessary things are few and easy, whereas non-necessary things are numerous, deceptive, fragile, difficult, and rarely honourable. Even if they were worthy of praise, we must recognize in ourselves what Pythagoras warned us about: that nothing outside of us truly belongs to us. Not only is it not ours, but nature did not intend for us, feeble creatures, to be guardians of anything other than ourselves, as it granted us only a small share of the use of a tiny part of its many things. And even if they were excellent and truly ours, let us acknowledge our mortality and the constant danger we face from many unpredictable events, never far from death. And even if we were to live as long as Nestor or any other who lived the longest, let us constantly remember, as the poet Manilius said:

"...labor gave intelligence to wretched mortals, and Fortune, by pressing, commanded each to keep watch over themselves."

And indeed, as Crisippus said, you will find no mortal who is not often confronted with things that cause them sorrow.

Therefore, we will acknowledge that the unpredictable nature of fortune can affect us just as it does other mortals, day by day. However, we will not allow this thought to fill us with sadness, as if we are constantly anticipating the downfall of our fortunes and circumstances. We will not excessively worry about every small change in the world around us, for as Augustus, the prince, wrote to Livia, that would only lead to a constant state of restlessness and inner turmoil. Instead, we will prepare ourselves and firmly commit to patiently endure whatever may come our way.

Even if something goes against our will, we will strive to align our judgment with the circumstances. We must remember that adversity can affect us just as it can affect anyone else. With the awareness of our mortality and the understanding that challenging situations can arise, let us follow the advice of the wise. They remind us to let the lessons of the past and present benefit future generations, and during times of prosperity, to prepare ourselves for the challenges that may lie ahead.

In this state of tranquility, we will learn to care less and almost forget about the injustices of fortune before they have a chance to harm us. Let us be inspired by the philosopher Bion, who, in his final moments, proudly proclaimed that he had never suffered anything against his will in his life. Through this gradual training, we will learn not to place excessive value and love on things beyond their deserving worth.

If you moderate your opinions and judgments, you will control your emotions and the movements of your mind. When love is moderated, desire diminishes. With extinguished desire, you will not feel the pain of lacking or having things that you do not value. They say, "Love your country, love your own and do good to them as they wish." But they also say that the world is the homeland of humankind, and that a wise person, wherever they may be, will make that place their own. They will not flee from their homeland, but adopt another and find great well-being where they have no harm, always avoiding being a burden to themselves. They praise the ancient saying of Teucer, a highly esteemed and wise man, who said that his homeland was wherever he thrived. Those things that bring contentment and peace to my mind are truly mine, but those that make me discontented and disturbed are not mine, but rather foreign and counted among our enemies. Furthermore, to eliminate any heaviness of the mind, it will be beneficial to avoid places, things, and people that are likely to cause us annoyance and disturbance.

In the midst of a multitude, you cannot stay or go without being jostled. This was the statement of the orator Crassus: the will of someone observed by many is not free. Solitude has always been a friend of tranquility, and this holds true when it is not idle. Idleness, no one doubts, nurtures every vice, and nothing disturbs more than vice. Ovid said, "Vices seize us if they are not shaken off like water."

The mind, naturally restless and diverse, is even more agitated than the waves. Therefore, solitude, combined with certain exercises that we will discuss later, can be beneficial. Just as we engage in various activities and take care of our bodies to satisfy our physical needs, we should also prioritize the well-being of our minds. Homer, the poet, noted that many troubles arise from our indulgence in satisfying our appetites, particularly those related to the belly, which ultimately lead to countless discomforts. Thus, let us not live solely for the gratification of our physical desires, but rather focus on fully utilizing our intellectual capacities. When we realize that attending to external matters requires us to be concerned with the interests of others as much as our own, we can allow the outcomes to be guided by the fortunes of those directly involved. However, this does not mean neglecting the health of our bodies; our aim should be to sustain them without indulging in excess. Diogenes, the cynic, humorously suggested that if simply scratching our bellies could satisfy hunger, we might do so, but we know that hunger torments us until we fulfill its demands. Apuleius, when accused, denied looking pale due to amorous pursuits but acknowledged that the exertion of his studies fatigued him. There are four factors that weaken and drain our natural vitality: pain, sleeplessness, unpleasant odors, and worries of the mind. I find it perplexing that as our bodies weaken, our minds also lose their freedom and independence. Therefore, we should provide our bodies with their essential needs and protect them from harmful influences that jeopardize our well-being. To prevent overburdening our minds with unnecessary concerns, we should avoid engaging in more than one task at a time, ensuring that each task is within our capabilities and not overly demanding. However, this does not mean dedicating all our time and effort solely to work and study. We should also allocate leisure time, allowing ourselves to relax and take breaks from intense mental exertion and unwavering focus. Asinius Pollio, a distinguished orator, as Seneca recounts, engaged in various demanding activities until the tenth hour of the day. Afterward, he indulged in leisure so extensively that he did not even read the letters sent to him by his friends. Our noble ancestors in Rome had a wise practice of prohibiting new business in the Senate after a certain hour, to provide space for leisure and tranquility amidst the numerous tasks. King Antiochus, after losing Asia, expressed gratitude to the Senate of Rome and felt relieved as his workload diminished. Yet, we, lacking prudence, not only burden ourselves with excessive busyness in our own affairs but also take on the affairs of others without being asked. There is an ancient proverb: "He who involves himself becomes entangled." It saddens me to witness the foolishness of many individuals who lack curiosity in cultivating virtue and instead never cease to pry into the words and actions of others. They resemble a persistent lover, as the charming poet Propertius writes:

"...once again, inquiring, he wearies the child, demanding more than she fears to know."

Perhaps it is necessary for me to intervene and introduce a matter unrelated to your leisure. Here, you should devote the same level of thought to not accepting it as you would if you were to undertake it. Aristotle argued in this manner: just as we endure war for the sake of peace, we undertake tasks to establish ourselves in leisure. We can only fulfill our needs by attending to them, and we seek what is beneficial to fulfill those needs. But nothing dishonorable can ever be necessary. Therefore, in order to live in honest leisure, we will undertake necessary exertions, not to agitate ourselves in ambition and ostentation. Hence, those who prioritize the affairs of the state among their foremost concerns and often abandon their own tasks to engage in the ambition of holding office seem to me to have misguided advice. When criticized, they respond that those who remain idle should continue to do so, believing that they are not truly men unless they are solicited and demanded by many. To me, they appear to lack prudence if they avoid finding contentment in themselves and, consequently, being free and happy. Galba, one of the twelve Roman emperors, used to say that no one would ever be forced to give an account of their leisure. And Epicurus attributed the supreme happiness of the gods to the fact that they have nothing else to do but contemplate themselves, which is not displeasing to me. I also agree with the statement of Crassus, who denied that a man could be considered free if he occasionally cannot do anything. In a ship, as Plato argues, if a capable and skilled individual is at the helm, what audacity would it be for someone else to remove them and take charge of the affairs? And if there is no capable person, why should it be you? Do you want to care more about public matters than all the others? But how will the reckless one, who cannot maintain tranquility and peace within themselves, govern others? How can they be considered more human? How can they govern an entire population and multitude? I will not dwell on this aspect. I will not recount the countless disturbances that ambition and the ostentation of our virtue, wisdom, and knowledge bring with them. Let us leave aside the envy that exists in others, for it certainly arises within us, leading to disputes and rivalries. Every dispute and competition carries sparks of conflict within it, which, when ignited, fuel intense hatred and enmity. "He loves the concern of victory," said Catullus. Indignation has always been associated with competitions and conflicts. Anger is a harmful thing in human life and is prone to greatly disturb our minds. For example, the Samian athlete Ateglies, born mute, upon being quickly awarded the prize and title of victory in the theater, was overcome with indignation, and his voice broke as he began to speak and express his sorrow. Cleopatra, scorned by Caesar Augustus, took her own life. Such is the power of anger within us, not only to stir up minds that are already predisposed to disturbance but also to distort and pervert every aspect and order of nature. But I will discuss this elsewhere.

Some people by nature are suspicious, harsh, and prone to anger. They should be avoided because just as someone else's fire warms our nearby walls, so does someone else's inflamed anger harm those who do not distance themselves by yielding and avoiding it. Especially those who are inactive, idle, and at the same time indulgent and slaves to their desires. First and foremost, informers and especially liars should be avoided, especially those who are deceitful and cunning. You will have nothing but reasons to complain and be outraged if you associate with such people. It is important to be slow to believe and convince yourself that every person is good. Anyone who speaks ill of others almost declares that they do not love them, and anyone who does not love those whom you consider good shows that you are an imprudent judge of others' virtues and, on the other hand, reveals themselves to be not good. They should not be trusted.

They say that wisdom enters through the ears, but from there, just like through the eyes, disturbance and turmoil also enter our minds. Therefore, close them off. There was someone who chose to live in blindness to better philosophize and to avoid seeing things that would distract them from their excellent thoughts and divert them from their constant investigations into the most hidden and rarest matters. I wouldn't dare criticize such a philosopher so much, but I also wouldn't know how to imitate them. I would find more delight in the story of Cotys, the prince to whom Plutarch recounts being presented with beautiful pottery vessels adorned with marvellous figures and frames. He accepted the gift with grace, admired and praised them greatly, and then broke them so as not to be upset if someone else were to break them. That's how we should be; and we will be like those judges in Venice who, when they consult to pronounce a verdict, present a tablet where they gather together and confer. In order to shield ourselves and hide from the many follies and annoyances of the common people and the insolent, we will present a book in which we will immerse ourselves. And since today everything that is said or done is often false and pretentious, we will first seek advice from ourselves and with time, regarding whether to believe or refute the words or actions of others. And we will scrutinize our own words more than anything else, for once a word is spoken, it cannot be taken back: if you remain silent, you can always choose not to speak. As Hippocrates said, silence does not cause thirst.

I won't go into detail here about how nature provided two valleys and hedges for our words, teeth and lips; and how it gave us two open and clear pathways for hearing. Let us please obey nature: we will listen from both sides; we will recognize that our speech is given to us not to detract from or incite discord and harm to others, but to transform our emotions, senses, and understanding for a good and happy life.

The ancients approved of a precept for living in pure tranquillity and peace of mind: never entertain the thought of doing something that you wouldn't want your friends and enemies to know. But I dare say this: those who are inclined to never speak the absolute truth will never hesitate to do something they would rather not reveal in the midst of a crowd, in the theatre. The value and utmost usefulness of truth in maintaining a steady calm, as well as its ability to hinder and disrupt us in deceit, should be discussed elsewhere.

Since we mentioned friends, we should take great care not to form close associations with those who seek to impose their own desires on you, where you would have to plead for your own needs. It is a golden maxim from our ancestors, as recounted by Seneca: nothing costs as much as what you acquire through pleading. Live happily with your equals. But follow the example of that... near the comic playwright Terence, who denied that anyone among his friends desired everything to be made known.

Strive to maintain goodwill but consider it a lesser connection than it once was, whenever possible.

Above all, I don't want to overlook this reminder: I tell you, Battista, avoid all dealings, schemes, and entanglements with any woman. According to Homer, the wise Agamemnon affirms that among mortals, there is no creature more wicked than a woman. All women are crazy and filled with fleas, and from them, you will only receive displeasure, trouble, and indignation. They are lustful, audacious, fickle, suspicious, stubborn, full of pretence, and cruelty.

By doing so day by day, closing off and blocking the path to disturbances in such a way that they find every entrance closed and every window sealed through which they might enter our minds, we will make every effort to live free and devoid of all annoyance. At the same time, we will study, as Alexander did, by training his people and fellow soldiers in every manoeuvre and movement necessary for skilful use of weapons against their enemies. Similarly, we will strive to train our bodies and senses in endurance and fortitude, which will make us steadfast and resolute against the vicissitudes of fortune and adverse circumstances. Our initial exercises will be focused on eliminating vices from our lives, as vices lead to the most obvious ruin of our souls.

In this regard, I believe we need to practice two things: moderating our desires and tempering our anger. We will provide both a method and restraint for achieving this if we establish the habit of caring less and less about our own pleasures and displeasures. We should be aware that we have successfully composed our minds for this task when we accept no contrary exceptions from ourselves. Today, the people gather for entertainment, but I choose to practice indifference towards this indulgence; I will retreat among my books and remain alone. If you have resolved to do the same, no persuasion from others, no thought will distract you from your purpose. However, the more you lend an ear or give credence to anything that leads you away from this intention, the less well-founded and prepared you will be to sustain yourself. And the less you resist your desires and give in to them, the more you will displease yourself, and the less you will be your own master or free. Extinguish and crush that thought. Refute any cause or condition that interrupts your devotion to virtue.

Amasis, the king of Egypt, wrote to Polycrates, a tyrant known for his incredible success, as recorded by the historian Herodotus. The message was as follows: "If there is anyone who genuinely wishes well for their friends, I am one of those individuals. I don't believe that you consider me a friend solely because of your own prosperity. However, it is evident that even the gods do not tolerate excessive happiness among mortals. Therefore, I have always believed it to be most advantageous to be prepared to endure both favourable and unfavourable circumstances. Those who have only experienced a life of constant happiness truly know nothing about the power of fortune. They lack the ability to think rationally, make fair decisions, or exercise unbiased judgment. Thus, if you trust me as a loyal and sensible friend, I urge you to consider my arguments against blind reliance on fortune. Let go of those things that are most precious to you and would cause you immense sorrow if lost. Learn how to endure pain and injustice during challenging times. Farewell."

This advice holds true for all of us. In our pursuit of wisdom, we can learn from the way music teachers teach dance to young students. They start by demonstrating the steps with accompanying music, guiding the inexperienced dancers to gradually make fewer mistakes. In a similar manner, although we may not achieve perfect harmony in our lives, we can adapt and adjust ourselves as we navigate through significant challenges. While acknowledging our imperfections, we should strive to transform ourselves each day, gradually becoming more virtuous and complete. As we diminish vices, virtues will flourish.

Some individuals are naturally inclined towards certain emotions that are not praiseworthy. Cinna was cruel, Sulla was impulsive and intense, and Marius remained perpetually angry. In such cases, we should train ourselves in small and insignificant matters to cultivate a different nature within us. Among philosophers, some would intentionally refrain from getting angry if others failed to please them or fulfil their requests. They would fervently and persistently ask statues for more favours. The philosopher Crates would purposely irritate the most lowly and vulgar women to practice listening to offensive and provocative words without being disturbed or upset. It is said that Epaminondas, a distinguished prince and a beacon of Greece, was given a menial task to provoke him, involving the maintenance of certain roads. He laughed and willingly undertook the assigned task. Similarly, you should find joy in situations that allow you to learn to overcome yourself.

The challenging circumstances of life provide us with an opportunity to develop virtue. Tigranes, the nephew of King Archelaus, spent an extended period in Rome, and in doing so, he shed his royal pomp and arrogance, becoming patient to the point of being servile. You have heard hurtful words from someone who dislikes you. You have experienced the arrogance of someone mocking you. In such situations, choose to endure it, or at least pretend to be patient. Consider it as a reciprocal act among friends, where serving others obliges them to serve you in return. By striving to please virtue, it will be ever-ready to support you, and you will find that by simulating, we can become what we aspire to be. A valuable strategy is to imitate those who remain undisturbed and untroubled. Plutarch believed that by controlling one's speech, anger can be extinguished. Therefore, it is highly beneficial to practice moderation in all aspects of life. Plato stated that the gods rewarded thoughtless and frivolous words with severe punishments. Scaurus refused to allow his enemy's servant to report the misdeeds of his own master. When Philip, the king of Macedonia, was excluded from his wife's chamber at night, he remained silent. Marcus Babius pardoned and set free the two soldiers, Gabbiani, who had killed his own son, Cleopatra. This is how a person who is well-advised, resolute, and steadfast behaves: they control and suppress the triggers of anger and disturbances. They find greater satisfaction in showing that they are not affected by anger when they could easily indulge in it.

Neither should anyone think that they can acquire any virtue without practicing and habituating it within themselves. Without writing or painting, you would never become a painter or writer. And even by writing, one does not learn to write well if they do not make an effort to avoid what made them write poorly. In order to align ourselves with virtue, we will undertake virtuous exercises, in which we engage with diligence through thinking, investigating, collecting, composing, commenting, and entrusting our efforts and vigilance to posterity. In doing so, we will distance and separate ourselves from every contamination and stain of vice, and we will live happily and contentedly. Oh, how sweet is the glory we acquire through our own efforts! Our labours are worthy, as they allow us to show to those who are not living alongside us that we have lived with evidence other than age. And to those who will come after us, we leave behind knowledge and a name that is more than just a stone inscription on our grave.

The poet Ennius said: "Do not weep for me, do not hold a funeral for me, for I will live on in the words of learned men."

But I don't intend to dwell solely on praising the exertion in praiseworthy and noble matters. I only wish to advise Battista on how important I believe it is to practice. As the poet Plautus said, "He who lives without occupations has more to do than the busy man; he goes up and down, not staying here or there, wandering and fighting with himself." And we, born into life like a ship, not to decay in the harbour but to sail long voyages at sea, will always strive, through practice, for some praise and fruit of glory. It will be beneficial to impose on ourselves the necessity of practicing virtue in this way. I once decided to study and comprehend everything Aristotle wrote in philosophy. I called upon some scholars and imposed on myself the task of reading his works for two hours every day. That self-imposed obligation made me more diligent than I probably would have been otherwise. Solinus writes that the deer teaches its young to run and flee. If the deer and other animals instinctively understand their needs and usefulness, why wouldn't we, as human beings, train ourselves accordingly? Therefore, in every aspect of living well, but especially in what is most necessary, we should dare above all to hate and avoid every vice that is close at hand. It is greatly beneficial to strive for the fame and immortality of one's name and memory. But above all, it is necessary to take good care of and cultivate the mind through proper education and worthy learning. The indulgence of bodily desires corrupts the mind and makes it vicious. Therefore, our primary and constant effort should be to practice a way of life that is content with few and easily attainable things.

Julius Capitolinus writes that Marcus Aurelius Antoninus, the ruler of the Roman Empire, slept on the ground to learn how to endure himself, and he did many other things similar to the philosopher Diogenes. It is said that Diogenes would embrace marble statues loaded with ice in the middle of winter just to dare himself to endure adverse conditions. The poet Silius praised Regulus in the following verses:

"He thought that enduring hardships, a drenched storm, meagre meals, and a hard bed, and competing with pressing enemies after conquering them was even greater than fleeing adversity by being cautious. He believed that it was more remarkable to overcome through endurance than to escape through caution."

Our Latin ancestors accustomed their young ones to a military and Spartan way of life, which was simple and without extravagance. It consisted of nothing more than bacon and cheese. They wanted them to be prepared for manly duties and free from servile entanglements. In the same way, we will train our bodies to be content with little and endure without delicacy. Through practice, we will achieve great things.

It is written that the doctors forbade moist things to Julius Viatore, a Roman knight, and he, daring himself, became someone who drank nothing in old age. Battista, here, used to experience great discomfort and disturbance in his health when he was unable to keep his head uncovered for as long as he worshipped during sacrifices. See him now, having become accustomed from one summer to another, unable to bear his head covered in the midst of the Alps and snow. What the art and care of doctors could not achieve, he can achieve through this habit. However, it is important to note that the power of habit in mortals extends beyond this example. The only remaining advice here is that if habit has the power to influence us, we must deviate from any habit that disturbs us due to the lack of something or the presence of something else, and focus on habits that provide us with little need for external help. The philosopher Diogenes refused to recall his runaway slave, as he wanted to test if he could live without his servant. If his servant could live without Diogenes, then Diogenes, even more so, should be able to live without a servant who had fled.

To many, the things I am recounting may seem difficult. However, they are not; they are easy for those who have the will to do so. Marcus Varro aptly said in his satires, "If you had invested only a twelfth of the effort you put into making your servant a good baker into adorning yourself, you would have become an excellent citizen long ago. Now you could sell that servant for a significant sum of money. Who would ever buy you at any price?" These exercises, for those who make the decision, are undoubtedly pleasant to experience because they feel themselves reaching higher levels of virtue with each endeavour. By trying them, they bring forth a happiness that one desires. And who wouldn't want to be free from the need for so many different things that life demands? For those who can lead their lives with few possessions, they require only a few things. First and foremost, in my opinion, true human freedom lies in being able to live without discomfort or annoyance with what is readily available. As the philosopher Solon said, "Among good things, we will need very little food in the second place when we do not need anything at all in the first place." Does it harm us that we were raised in the lap of our mother and in the delights and indulgences of our father, and now fortune provides us with abundant resources, making us feel that such austerity in living does not suit our grand lifestyle? This is where we need to take action. I say, remember that we are human beings exposed to all circumstances; you know that times change, and fortunes are fickle. In times of prosperity, we must prepare ourselves to withstand misfortune. Those who have not learned to endure, Niccolo, do not know how to suffer, but those who have learned, they know and benefit from it. Chilon, a philosopher, responded to his brother, who was upset for not being chosen as one of the magistrates called Ephors, even though Chilon had been in that position multiple times: "Oh my brother, do not be surprised if our fellow citizens do not treat you as they do me. You do not know how to endure insults, but I have learned not to care by enduring them." Octavia, the sister of Britannicus, writes Cornelius, even from a young age, learned to hide pain, show charity, and suppress all emotions. It benefitted her, and it was a worthy and necessary education for a prince amidst so much abundance and freedom, to learn self-moderation and self-control. In Arabia, where the pastures are lush, as Curzio writes, shepherds separate and limit the sheep from grazing too much, as excessive food would make them sick. And indeed, as Caesar said according to Sallust, among the greatest evils, we must consider excessive freedom. Therefore, we will question and limit ourselves as much as possible, desiring less than what we are capable of in all other aspects except in acquiring virtue and earning glory.

Solon said that wealth breeds satiety, and satiety leads to contempt, and from contempt, we see the desire for revenge. We must dare to value these riches and abundance less, distancing ourselves from them by spending them on worthy and commendable things. We should first give them away, almost depositing them among the virtuous and the learned, because what you give, fortune cannot take away, and what fortune may take from you will not burden you. In addition to this, we must train ourselves to forget minor offenses so that we can endure and forget the major ones in due time. Antisthenes, the philosopher, believed that there was no better discipline in life than unlearning the memory of offenses. Aristotle denied that it was a noble and strong-minded act to constantly remind oneself, especially of unpleasant things. For this reason, Themistocles desired to learn from Simonides not his art of remembering but rather some art of forgetting.

If we want to achieve all these things, we must train ourselves gradually, from one thing to another and over time. It is necessary to exert effort over time, and in our exertions, we need tolerance; in tolerance, we need strength, and in strength, we require wisdom and reason. In all our actions, we should align ourselves with justice and humanity, finding great pleasure in every virtue we acquire. As Aristotle said, the pleasure of exertion brings about a good outcome in every endeavour. King Amasis of Egypt once replied that anything done with pleasure is effortless.

I don't want to overlook one important point: for every excellent institution, for every good reason to live, for every refinement and adornment of our souls, it will greatly benefit us to engage in literature, to acquire knowledge and expertise in the art of memory and admonitions, which scholars have recommended to future generations. Just as a hand gently softens and prepares wax to receive the impression and seal of a gem, so do letters mold the mind for every duty and the pursuit of glory and immortality.

What do you think, Niccolo, about what we have discussed so far? Have you seen the ways in which we need to prepare ourselves and conduct our lives in order to exclude disturbances that can invade and occupy our minds? Now, let us explore what arguments and techniques can help us cleanse our hearts of resentment and anxiety. But I feel unqualified for such an endeavor. I know that what

I presented would require careful consideration. I shared what came to mind in our conversation, without order and perhaps with some confusion. I did it solely to challenge your claim that you desired useful advice from scholars regarding this matter. Did you not see, as in other aspects of a good and happy life, that they were not negligent and fulfilled all our needs and expectations?

NICCOLO: I saw it, and I am pleased. But here, Battista and I would like to ask and urge you to continue showing us, as you mentioned earlier, the art and arguments that can alleviate the anxieties already conceived in our minds.

AGNOLO: We shall see.

BOOK II

You saw in the previous book the importance of premeditation and mental discipline in order to exclude and prevent disturbances, and I believe it satisfied you. You saw how concisely it gathered a wealth of excellent reminders and teachings from our wise and prudent ancestors. In this book, you will learn how, if you find yourself already burdened by sadness, grief, or any other emotional turmoil, you can reasonably and effectively purge it and restore equanimity and tranquillity to your mind and soul.

Agnolo Pandolfini, a highly learned and eloquent man, engaged in a discussion with Niccolò, Messer Veri de' Medici, who is among the foremost scholars in Tuscany, combining great wisdom with immense affability. The following incident took place: the morning after our previous conversations, Niccolò and I were at our main temple to pay homage to the sacrifice, and when we saw each other, we greeted one another warmly. Agnolo was accompanied by two messengers from the highest magistrates. Upon reaching us, Agnolo greeted us and said, "These messengers are requesting and urging me to go up to the Palazzo to counsel with the other fathers for the sake of our homeland and the public good. May the immortal God and the other inhabitants and governors of the heavens bear witness to my will and dedication. Nothing occupies my mind or resides in my thoughts more than preserving and enhancing the authority, dignity, and majesty of my homeland, while also ensuring the welfare and reputation of every private citizen. But what kind of perversity would it be if, called upon to give counsel, we were compelled to say not what we believe to be useful, honourable, and necessary in these times and conditions of our lives and fortunes, but rather what we think would please those who ask? The nature of human beings is twisted in many ways, and it is worthy of criticism. We see wild animals born to be impetuous, ravenous, and completely untamed, and yet they will never harm each other unless provoked and incited by some frenzy. We humans, on the other hand, who are born to be modest, gentle, and agreeable, always seem to strive to be stubborn, troublesome, and hostile towards others. And if this is madness, anyone who advises to add to it would, as that poet said, wish to go mad with some reason. They kept me until late last night, and now they demand my presence again. I won't have time to be here for several hours when you may need me. And if I were to be of assistance to you, I wouldn't wait to be asked. Therefore, let us use this time for something else, and perhaps we will be of service to someone else. For if I were to speak up there about what I truly feel, it would not benefit me, and if I were to say something I don't believe, it would not please others.

So Agnolo said to us, then he turned to the two messengers and sent them to the higher authorities with a valid excuse. He then turned to Niccolò, smiled, and said, "Where were you headed? Perhaps to exercise, huh? Well done. Exercise and moderation, two excellent things, preserve health, maintain youthfulness, and prolong life. These beautiful sunsets invite us to enjoy the pleasantness of our delightful surroundings. I wish, Battista, we could be down there in our Gangalandi with the dogs, or in the hills or plains, and exercise for a while, and then return to our studies of literature and philosophy, as is your custom, Battista. But if you agree, Niccolò, and if you have some free time, let's take a stroll towards the Servi. We'll go around San Marco and come back here. How does that sound?" This is what Agnolo said.

Niccolò replied, "Nothing delights Battista as much as exercise. I have often seen him, especially during the rainy winter days when we couldn't go out, leave his books and exercise with a ball, performing various movements and showing agility. On dry days, it was rare for him not to climb up the steep hill to pay his respects at the temple of San Miniato. And as for his exercises in the countryside, you can see them for yourself, Agnolo, as you live nearby. And certainly, if I had a building as suitable and magnificent in such a pleasant and healthy place as yours, Agnolo, I wouldn't know where to spend most of my days other than there. So, for Battista, who enjoys exercising, I have no doubt that he would enjoy what you suggested. Our intention was also to be with you wherever it pleased you, not only to accompany you, for being in your company, esteemed and dignified gentleman, brings us reverence and grace, but also because we take pleasure in being with you to seek and obtain what you promised to tell us today, regarding the moderation and arrangement of our minds to live free and undisturbed. We are not only idle but also eagerly interested in hearing from you and following your guidance. Let's go then."

AGNOLO: Am I, as they say, removing a burden from my shoulders only to put it on my head? I relieved myself of the burden of those who wanted me at the Palazzo, and I came to you to take on an even greater responsibility. I did promise you something, and I prepared myself in advance for what I should discuss with you. But what can we talk about that is more relevant to these times and our current public situation than this one thing that makes us free and immune to every agitation and disturbance of the mind? I do not refuse to satisfy you to the best of my abilities. And my discourse will be a kind of exploration and commentary with you on what is beneficial. If we direct our attention to something useful and fitting, our efforts will be worthwhile, for indeed, as Crisippus said and as those who have experienced it know, sorrows, sadness, and other troubles of the mind are much greater and more intense than those of the body. And how many things have been investigated and continue to be tested to heal the body? Who would blame us for seeking and embracing every reasonable argument to heal and restore the mind to its natural state of wholeness? But, as they say, "nihil dictum quin prius dictum," what new thing can we bring forth that has not been heard and told by many others? We will relate what comes to mind from one thing to another, and perhaps in many instances, some will resonate with us. And just as for bodily ailments, a single method of treatment suffices, so for the maladies of the mind, perhaps a single remedy will be enough.

But where shall we begin? Shall we explore the countless disturbances of the mind, a task neither easy nor small? If, as they say, every disturbed mind experiences a kind of insanity, and there are infinite varieties of madness, then there will also be infinite disturbances. Biante the philosopher considered it a form of illness for the mind to desire impossible things. I laugh. And let us, Niccolò, consider whether our desire to deal with the impossible with our feeble intellects is a manifest illness of the mind. It may be wiser for us to acknowledge our limitations and focus on what is within our reach.

NICCOLA: It is written among the poets that Silenus taught Midas not to fear death. I won't mention Plato and others like him who have benefited those who listened to their admonitions and reminders. Similarly, I have no doubt that with your abundant knowledge, as you demonstrated yesterday, you will be able to help and satisfy us. This task should not be difficult or beyond your capabilities. We have already witnessed greater proofs of your intellect, and we beseech you and eagerly await your response.

AGNOLO: What was I thinking just now? Whenever we are free from sorrow, we are pained by the sorrows of others; and when we are overwhelmed by grief, we find solace in the misfortunes of others and draw comfort from their sufferings. Hence the desire for vengeance, punishment, and retribution. Where does this come from?

NICCOLA: We are attentive and interested, Agnolo. Please continue. You are acting like Darius in Asia, who scattered gold, gems, and precious objects as he fled, in order to distract and delay those pursuing him. Likewise, you are now introducing new questions to divert us from what you promised, worthy though they may be, but they should be considered elsewhere. We implore you, grant us this favour. Let all the jesting you have done thus far serve as an introduction to this subject.

AGNOLO: So be it, if that's what you desire, and may God grant it. Very well, let me summarize one of our divisions from yesterday on this subject. We said that disturbances arise and persist in our minds either from the turmoil of the times, the harshness of our fortune, some unfortunate event, the malice and insolence of the people we interact with in life, or from our own imprudent words or actions. That was our division yesterday. Let us add another point, that there are remedies that help with not just one, but multiple disturbances. Some remedies are effective for one type of disturbance but not as much for another. Thus, we will first present specific remedies for each ailment that are suitable and well-adapted to eliminate and eradicate any lingering resentment and animosity within us. Then we will gather together all the remedies that we deem capable of calming and extinguishing any disruptive agitation and fury that may have been aroused in our minds and thoughts. We will begin by treating those bruises and wounds of the soul that our imprudence and rashness have caused in us.

Here, we must not overlook a common and grave error made by many, who consider themselves to be leading a peaceful and tranquil life as long as fortune and favourable circumstances align with their desires and wishes. They fail to realize that they are bound in the midst of vehement oppressions and then consider themselves victims of fortune and burdened by adversity, when in fact they themselves are the source of their own troubles and distress. And here we have the example of someone, a most fortunate individual, who takes pleasure in their home, their villa, their possessions; who values status, dignity, and power more than anything else; who finds delight in their spouse and takes joy in becoming a parent; who takes pride in the good qualities and future prospects of their offspring. Oh, the vanity of mankind! Oh, how poorly balanced is reason! These, mortals, these are the poisons of the soul for you. From here arises that which corrupts the true and worthy masculinity in our hearts, and then, having become effeminate, we no longer tolerate ourselves and blame the innocence of others for our own mistakes. It was excessive love for this or that thing, excessive indulgence in various pleasures, the seed and spark of such an intrusive flame that ignites anger and causes you to grieve over having left behind and lost what once pleased you so much.

To someone who wanted to flee their homeland and go into exile, Socrates said, "Rather, by my advice, flee this moroseness of your soul, which makes you ill at ease wherever you may be." Therefore, let us first rid ourselves of these attachments and desires that are the roots and source of so much anxiety and torment. Let us set them aside by aligning ourselves with truth and obeying reason. They will show you how to recognize the volubility and inconstancy of those you love, and they will reveal that the affection of those who present themselves as friends is tied to you only as long as the bond that compelled you to love each other lasts. For if it was some utility or pleasant reason for living together in joy and merriment that bound you together in such close union, do not let yourself be persuaded that fortune will always be fair and favorable between you. And do not doubt that there will be times for you, as there have been and will continue to be for all mortals, as is the custom and nature of things. Observe how they have varied and changed from hour to hour. Thus, you will recognize that these fortunes of yours, this beauty and grace of your youth and form, whenever they may be, will pass away like things lost and extinguished.

Therefore, do not place such hope in your expectations that you exclude every reason and counsel that could make you doubt and foresee within yourself what can and often does happen to others with its weight and sadness. Look, here are your father and these children, here are your fellow citizens and many friends, some closely connected to you, countless acquaintances and interactions, here are riches equal to a king, greatness, authority, dignity, everything that can be desired among mortals. Oh, you, miserable and unhappy person, if perhaps you possess everything else but do not possess yourself. And do not think that you possess yourself where you cannot control yourself much more in prosperous circumstances than in adverse ones. And not always, no, does the son remain the heir to the father; nor do I know if there have been more parents and mothers who mourned their offspring than there have been children who wept for their parents. And as for these friends of ours, who will assert that they bring us more pleasure than sorrow in life? Valerius Martial said it well: "Be not too friendly to anyone: you will love less, and you will grieve less as well."

Oh, the most pernicious plague to mortals, excessive love! Pliny writes that Publius Catinæus Philotimus, having been left as the sole heir to the fortunes of his master whom he served and loved deeply, out of an excessive desire for his deceased master, threw himself into the midst of the fire where the body was being cremated and honoured. It was an act of impotent and furious spirit. But let us discuss elsewhere the frenzies that still drive miserable mortals, burning in excessive love. As for the certainty and stability of our hopes and contentments, let those who hope and enjoy more than they ought consider it. This is a reminder I would give to anyone willing to listen, that in considering their own reasoning and purpose in this matter, they should also take into account the hardships and melancholies that are mixed and sprinkled among their many pleasures and delights. And who does not see that every human pleasure, except for that which is placed in pure and simple virtue, is always filled with infinite suspicions, fears, and sorrows, now of not attaining, now of losing what delighted and satisfied them? Virgil says in relation to Aeneas fleeing from his burning and ruined homeland Troy, carrying his father on his back and leading his son by the hand, it was not his armed enemies but his dearest ones who disturbed him. The charming poet says: "For neither enemy weapons nor Greeks massed in opposing battle array had ever troubled me; now every breath of wind frightens me, every sound makes me start and tremble, fearing for myself and for those who accompany me and for my burden."

But I will not go into demonstrating here that joy and hope are, in themselves, disturbances and ailments of the soul no less than fear and sorrow. That discussion can take place elsewhere. It is enough to have shown you, in passing, that in order to live a quiet and tranquil life, we must moderate and restrain ourselves in every pleasure and in the fulfilment of our opinions and expectations. And if, due to some inconsiderate and immoderate word or action on our part, or due to some past negligence and inertia, we become disturbed, let us not be ungrateful for that remorse through which we learn to hate and avoid all immodesty and intemperance. And if, as the poet Catullus says, to each his own error is attributed, but no one sees how thin his own back is, it benefits us sometimes to have erred where we then recognize ourselves as frail and no more divine than other mortals. And thus, let there be in us a certain incentive and stimulus to deserve better through our industry and diligence. "Pain and tears made me eloquent," said the poet Propertius. And how many, because they were disgusted by their past bad habits, have become adorned with virtue and a virtuous life! The historian Aelius Spartianus writes that the emperor Hadrian, ridiculed in the Senate for delivering a speech with excessive triviality, resolved to improve himself and, with assiduity and diligence, became an excellent orator. And not without reason did Petronius Thrasea, as recorded by the historian Cornelius, say that all the excellent laws and honourable examples among the virtuous originated from the offenses and failures of the non-virtuous. Therefore, one should not only, as said by... near Terence, correct one's own life through the lives of others but, first and foremost, from our own lives and conduct, we should daily draw inspiration and strive for a better state of mind and soul, succeeding in improving ourselves and finding joy in every acquisition and growth in virtue and praise.

We spoke about the disturbances that arise within us, originating from ourselves. Now, let us explore how we can keep our minds calm and tranquil, even if we are provoked and mistreated by the injustice and wickedness of others. But before we delve into this, it is important to understand that we often believe we are not at fault, yet we frequently err and bring upon ourselves turmoil and grave distress due to our inconsiderate reasoning and imprudence. Similarly, we often feel offended by others when we ourselves are the authors and instigators of our own discontent.

Niccola, do you think it is easy for us mortals to avoid and not be affected by envy when it arises from various sources, whether it be from observing and hearing about others or from recognizing it within ourselves? Oh, envy is a grave disturbance indeed! Your dear Leonardo, a most noble and beloved man, Battista, wrote extensively about its power in his tragic work, Hiensale, which he prepared for this illustrious second poetic competition, an excellent institution that serves the name and dignity of our homeland, designed to inspire the most brilliant minds and suitable for the cultivation of good morals and virtues. Oh, he is a shining light of our times! An ornament to the Tuscan language! It is through this platform that all the excellence and glory of our citizens flourished. However, I fear, Battista, that you may not be able to present your works; envy holds great influence in our current age, along with human malice. What no one can help but praise and approve, many seek to denounce and criticize. My fellow citizens, will you always be unjust to those who truly love you? You must certainly support talented minds and better reward the virtuous, which you have failed to do. Are these not the fruits of the vigilance and efforts of those who strive to benefit you? As for the challenges of envy and the troubles encountered in the world of literature, they shall be discussed elsewhere. Battista, continue with every endeavor and diligence to be of service to your fellow citizens. There will be those who love and appreciate you after we are gone, if these individuals offend you.

For now, let us establish that envy harms both public and private matters in many ways. It is a hidden evil that infects and grips us before we even sense its traps. Envy arises not only from what others possess in abundance but also from what we may lack within ourselves. It also emerges from our misguided opinions, insatiable desires, and lust. Envy can even exist in the hearts of those who consider themselves wise and prudent, those who deem themselves just and righteous. They judge as unworthy of such fortunes anyone who appears modest and too restrained in offering help and gratitude. They believe their own pain is justified when they lack what others possess abundantly. They do not measure their own advantages against what is necessary, nor do they weigh their abundance against genuine need. Instead, they determine these matters not by reason but by their will and intemperate appetite. They desire not what would truly contribute to their well-being and happiness but rather what appears desirable to them, for any reason, just or unjust. Often, these desired things would not benefit them if acquired or harm them if not obtained.

Thus, we find ourselves blinded by the torches of envy, unable to discern how these negative emotions within us are not driven by reason but rather by disturbance and perversity of mind. You have heard about Filippides, who ran from Athens to Sparta in just two days, covering a distance of 240 stadia. And you read about Philonius, Alexander's messenger, who, spurred by Sitione, arrived at Elim on the same day, covering a distance of 305 stadia. And you came across Strabo's account, cited by Varro, of witnessing the incredible sight of an army leaving the harbour of Carthage from a great distance. They say that Herodes was such a skilled hunter and fighter that he was unmatched, and in a single day, he killed about 40 wild animals. Perhaps you too would like to possess similar abilities. Maybe you would even wish to fly over the waters like Icarus or traverse the highest wheat stalks like the legendary Pantasilea. If nature were here as the procurer of things, ready to fulfil your every just desire, I believe you would perish from asking for such immoderate and excessive things. And even if you were to ask, it would respond, "What I have given you is enough to live a joyful and contented life. I have bestowed upon you a body more beautiful than other animals, movements that are agile and versatile beyond your imagination, acute senses that are sharp, alert, and clear. You possess intellect, reason, and memory equal to the immortal gods. These other dishonourable things, unsuited for bliss and happiness, how could they make you better or more steadfast in virtue? And if they cannot make you better, how could they ever truly satisfy you?"

Therefore, let us acknowledge our mistake and not persist in the disturbance of trying to compensate for what we perceive as ill-gotten in others and desiring it for ourselves when it is unnecessary, believing ourselves driven not by envy but by just and free indignation. Once we recognize that our wrongdoing stems solely from our misguided opinions, it will be easier for us to correct ourselves and find greater peace.

It also happens that, often being too lenient towards our own mistakes, we bring upon ourselves heaviness and bitterness. We feel hurt if someone dares to narrate or preach about what we ourselves were unable to refrain from saying or doing, acting without reason and hasty will. If what others speak of you is not flattering, blame yourself for giving them reason and material to speak in such a manner. Blame those who erred in the past, not those who speak the truth now. As Euripides, the tragic poet, stated in the words of Agamemnon, "You who dared to sin must bear with an undisturbed spirit many ungrateful things." Furthermore, excessive greed for praise and an overwhelming desire to be honoured and esteemed are fraught with great disturbance. We must not forget what the wise say, that seeking to please many is nothing more than wanting to displease the good and the wise. It should be enough for us to acquire fame and pursue glory among the common people through our efforts and vigilance, as long as we are satisfied with our own leisure. We should consider those who genuinely praise and esteem us as affirming our righteousness, temperance, and virtue. As for criticisms and tales that may arise to our detriment from our rivals, envious ones, and enemies, we should aspire to possess such maturity that we establish within ourselves a spirit that cares more about being good and knowledgeable than about appearing so in the eyes of others. It is said that to a wise person, their conscience is a grand and renowned theatre. The wise person seeks no other judges of their life and actions than themselves. Bion, the philosopher, added to these sentiments that a truly virtuous person should be willing to hear derogatory remarks from others about themselves, without reacting negatively, as if a comedy were being performed on a stage. I do not deny that, as they say, we should learn gentleness from the harassment of our enemies in order to live happily and joyfully with good friends. And certainly, when it requires a strong spirit, it is better to endure harsh words from others with a calm and unruffled mind than to seek revenge with a troubled soul. I would praise those who can restrain themselves and moderate the impulses and movements of their own spirit. However, in the world we live in today, as that comic poet said, "One man is a wolf to another." Perhaps, against offenses, we must both feel and refute them and seek revenge.

The greatest revenge one can take is to make those who speak ill of you liars through your good deeds. It would be a rare and supreme form of revenge if those who wish to say nothing about you were compelled to praise you greatly, and those who wish to criticize you were unable to do so. Cicero wrote to Dolobella, saying, "May your spirit be strong and wise in such a way that your moderation and dignity shame the insults of others." And Planco wrote to Cicero, "In this regard, I find pleasure in the fact that the more my enemies hate me, the more it pains them to be unable to blame me." Socrates, offended by those poets, laughed and said, "With your clever verses, you shed light on every aspect of my life, and by biting me, you reveal your own wounds and the nature of my virtue. Now, some will take notice of my character, whom they previously disregarded, and others will love me when they recognize my true virtue beyond what they hear. I, like a rock in the middle of the sea, persist in enduring your insults, and through my endurance, I conquer. The more boldly you taunt me, the more you will break yourselves, and the more bitterly you will regret it." Let us follow the same path: through patience and enduring the insolence of others, we will prevail. Let us emulate the orator Antony, who, it is said, by restraining himself, made those who provoked him with immoderate words appear completely furious. Marcus Octavius subdued the furious outbursts of Tiberius Gracchus through tolerance. According to the historian Josephus, King Agrippa of Jerusalem stated that the one who is offended and suffers easily induces a sense of shame in the offender for persisting in their malice. Numa, the king of the Romans, diverted his citizens from the use and practice of arms to the worship and observance of religion, thereby reducing their hostility and troubles caused by their neighbours, and he gained their love and reverence. Sometimes, it is necessary to learn how to lose, as there is gain in that loss which leads to a future where you lose less.

But if perhaps these adversaries and enemies of yours continue to plague you with their insults and malice, I am not someone who desires anything inhumane from a human soul. Julius Capitolinus writes that Antoninus Pius said to those who forbade weeping in his presence, "Let him be human, for the emotions of the soul cannot be taken away by command or completely suppressed by any philosophy." So, I do not forbid you from feeling the bitter things that humans feel when you yourself are human. An ancient Greek proverb states, "He who does not feel insults is more than six times a cow." And as those Tarquins used to say, as Livy the historian records, it is indeed perilous to live among mortals without anything other than innocence. Sometimes it is necessary to show that your heart feels anger just like that of your companion. A person with an unsteady and unclear eye responded to a hunchback and lame person, saying, "You spoke well, for I see poorly when I considered you upright and equal." And so shall we. To prevent others from further erring and to avoid falling into the trap, as the poet Laberius said, where frequent offense turns patience into fury, we will shake off and distance ourselves from those who are too persistent in biting and insolence, so as not to succumb to bursting with excessive resentment later on. I would prefer not to always be that corner where every difficulty is resolved. But I want to serve modesty in this regard, and I interpret that saying of Xenophon, who said that one rarely regrets winning, in a better light than you may think. Those who lose nothing already triumph over their ill-wishers to a great extent, and you would lose yourself if you were to plunge into premature anger and resentment. Do not give in to wrath but reserve yourself for some temperate and suitable occasion and time to satisfy yourself, where you can demonstrate your capabilities and strength in due time. Meanwhile, like in a trap, restrain yourself, as Socrates did according to Plato, when he was bitten by abusive words in Gorgias by ..., he did not respond immediately, but after much reflection, when the opportunity arose, he acknowledged his merit and reproached him in a gracious manner, saying, "What will you do when you are old if you cannot remember this now in your youth?" Similarly, we, where only words are needed, it will be beneficial to vent ourselves once, to pour out all our impulses, as Cicero did in the case of Vatinius as a witness. And then, once the blaze is extinguished and the fire has evaporated, we must recall and gather ourselves. And where perhaps something more than words is needed, Niccolo, insults are a bad thing, but it is not advisable to respond with anger and impetuosity, but rather with counsel and maturity. With slow counsel, actions are done quickly. Anger is the enemy of all counsel because anger is a brief madness, and madness does not go well with deliberation. And the shortest path to satisfy yourself will be the one that is secure.

Those noble Sabines, deceived by the Romans and stripped of their rights, sought revenge for the bitter injury inflicted upon their wives and daughters. They did not act with rage or ostentation, but with reason and composure. They prepared themselves in such a way that, when the time came, they broke free with great determination and armed force. Those who had offended them recognized them as men of honour, worthy of respect, and undeserving of such injustice and contempt. Similarly, we will not rush into our affairs, but we will handle them with composure and aim for a better outcome. And if time and opportunity do not align with our desires, we will not harbour eternal wounds like Juno, as described by the poet Virgil. Instead, we will heed the advice of the wise Phoenix, as portrayed by Homer, who said to Achilles, "Tame your unruly spirit, for the gods, who undoubtedly surpass you in virtue and dignity, are flexible." We will tame ourselves, leaning more towards ease and indulgence than severity and austerity. And perhaps it will not be uncommon to follow the example of Agrippina, who, upon realizing the danger lurking in the ship set up by Nero to crush and destroy her, found it useful and the only remedy for her troubles to pretend ignorance and forget. The ultimate and best resolution to any offense has always been to forget it. And even if the conceived resentment taints us to the point where forgetting is impossible, we will at least conceal or disguise it. According to the historian Curtius, Eustemon, one of the four thousand Macedonians captured and mutilated by the Persians, when they debated whether they should return to Greece in their disfigured state without noses, eyes, and hands, said, "Those who hide their miseries endure them well; for the afflicted, their homeland is solitude. No one loves those who cause them discomfort. Calamity is querulous, and happiness is proud. Each person advises based on their own fortune when deliberating on another's fortune. If we were not collectively miserable, we would be a burden to one another. It is no wonder that the fortunate seek their equals in fortune." These words are worth remembering, which is why I have shared them with you.

But as for us and our needs, this is what we will do: we will seek counsel from our own fortune, and in times of adversity, we will not be querulous, and in the hopeful prospect of seeking revenge, we will not be rigid or arrogant. In the meantime, we will conceal our hardships, awaiting a suitable opportunity and place to satisfy ourselves. We will emulate what Hannibal did, as described by the poet Silus, upon hearing of his brother's death:

"He suppresses his tears... and conquers his misfortunes by enduring them steadfastly, while he secretly murmurs about offering long-delayed funeral rites to his brother."

And if you feel pain and cannot bear it within yourself, and perhaps you recognize yourself as described by the poet Tibullus, when he said:

"I am not strong in this, nor does my patience match the strength of my heart; grief breaks the strongest spirits."

Then we will do as Odysseus did, as depicted by Homer, when a bard sang at a feast, potentially unpleasant things to him. Odysseus covered his head and wept; then, after the song ended, he uncovered himself and showed his joy by drinking to the gods' favor. Similarly, we will yield to our vulnerability as much as possible, keeping it hidden and concealed. But why do we seek wisdom in these recollections? Where else can we find more relevant and instructive lessons than from Homer, the truly divine poet, who so skilfully and gracefully depicted how one should navigate through life? He wrote about how Odysseus faced various challenges: he observed the customs of many men and the traditions of numerous cities; he travelled to distant lands and endured countless hardships in life, amidst weapons, on the sea's tumultuous waves, with such wisdom and discernment that he gained a renowned name and immortal fame. Thus, it is affirmed that he was the most prudent and experienced of all. Let us, therefore, recognize his actions in order to better follow in his footsteps when the need arises.

After enduring numerous shipwrecks, Odysseus returned to his homeland, unrecognized and poorly dressed. He found his house transformed into what resembled a public tavern, filled with lascivious and immodest people who squandered and consumed all his possessions. He was saddened and decided to seek revenge. However, he restrained himself and said to himself, "Oh heart, that has endured hardships elsewhere, hold firm." Someone even kicked Odysseus, yet he remained calm and silent, pretending to be like a fool, extending his hand and politely begging each person in the room, which was the same room where he had once received and honoured the princes of Greece. Again, he was struck with a stool, and he remained quiet and steadfast, without uttering a word or making any gesture, almost like a stone, only moving his head slightly. Those reckless troublemakers wanted him to fight against the despicable Irontes, who wanted to drive Odysseus out of his own home. Odysseus did not refuse, but instead of using his full strength, he gave him a light punch, so as not to hinder his greater plan. Then Ethisippus threw a bull's shinbone to strike Odysseus on the head, and Odysseus, remaining calm, simply inclined his head. Oh, the incredible patience in one man, an unheard-of and rare steadfastness! Oh, an example worthy of remembrance among mortals! In his own house, treated with insolence even by fools, humiliated, struck, and rejected, Odysseus never revealed himself through words or gestures. He endured all their drunkenness, disguised his anger, played along with their games and torment, silently and patiently enduring everyone's insults, because that was his purpose. He alone was surrounded by that large and bestial group. He was not yet ready to seek revenge, while they were eager and ready to heap insults upon him. He could not reveal himself without extreme danger, nor could he leave without unbearable sadness and bitterness. They were merry and intoxicated there, while many others were present, making them seemingly invincible. Therefore, Odysseus decided to endure and wait, dissimulating, hoping that time or the foolishness of those who had wronged him would bring an opportunity and a suitable place for retribution and revenge. Only towards Melancum, Penelope's handmaiden, who plagued Odysseus with insolent and feminine words, did he turn with a grave expression and a terrifying gaze, which frightened her. The wise Odysseus did not want to provoke her any further, as he could easily dismiss her without disrupting his plan. He acted like Ammonius Plutarchus, who does not willingly offer himself to troubles and sorrows unless necessary. But when the situation is fitting, it is our duty not to refuse any opportunity that allows us to act virtuously. And so, Odysseus proceeded. Finally, when the time came, that group, drenched in wine, exhausted from laughter, and weary from indulgence, encountered Odysseus, who was ready and sober, armed with his bow. First, he tested the string, inspected every part of it, and prepared himself and his arrows for what was to come. He did not want to neglect anything that might compromise his success due to negligence or impulsive desire for revenge. Then you see how he displayed his courage and skill against those who had treated him poorly.

We should do the same. If we truly intend to satisfy our anger completely, we will approach it with mature deliberation, address what is necessary, endure patiently, and exhibit strength and steadfastness when the opportunity arises for us to seek satisfaction. In all our decisions, we will exclude haste and impulsive desires. Just as a fruit arrives in due time and even the hardest and slowest to ripen endure their own season, let us hope for the fulfillment of your desires when they are just. The heavens favor righteous endeavors. Meanwhile, calm yourself and do not add new stimuli and resentment to your pain. Reflect repeatedly on how necessary this undertaking is for you. What you could have declined and refused to do was not necessary. But perhaps you perceive this offense and measure it against your own life, weighing it with your own principles. Oh, how sweet our existence would be if all mortals were good and resembled you! But perhaps you argue thus: "I have never done this, nor will I ever do it." You would not take Dametas' goat, nor would Dametas take Atteon's hunting dog, nor would Atteon take Plato's prized Pythagorean books. Each person is drawn by their own desires. Furthermore, necessity holds even greater sway, and the allure and habit of living entice our minds toward various customs and ways of life. But let us not digress. The offense must be diminished to the degree that the offender added reason or circumstances that compelled them to act and treat you in that manner. Codrus was poor, yet he accepted from Crassus. Marcus Caelius was handsome, yet he yielded to the passions for Clodia. Likewise, in comparing and weighing all these considerations, you may find that the offense appears greater due to the timing, the place, and the person who you loved and whom you constantly obliged with your kindness and favour. Do not dwell on this, as every moment is unrelated, and every place unworthy of injustice. And if, as they say, nothing is bitter to us unless we consider it so, and your troubles are not caused by others' foolishness but reside in your own perception, let him who acted rashly and immoderately bear the blame, not you the pain. When the opportunity arises to seek revenge, what greater vengeance than to make him repent for having offended someone he shouldn't have? It is easier to achieve this revenge by benefiting those who have wronged you rather than confronting them with offenses. It would be a most gratifying and praiseworthy act to offer this new grace to an old friendship, and it would be a noble act of leadership to establish new goodwill through this rare act of kindness. But regardless of your thoughts, I remind you that in all your deliberations and decisions, do not let yourself be swayed by turmoil. Just as a sailor adjusts their course when the wind pushes from one side, oppose it and stand firm on the other. Do not always favor your own cause but confirm within yourself every reason and excuse of those who have displeased you. In this way, you will navigate through the waves and storms of life, balanced and secure.

We have discussed the troubles that arise from within ourselves and the offenses and injustices we receive from other people. Now, let us investigate the reasons and methods to calm and pacify the disturbances that arise within us due to the common times, circumstances, and fortunes we encounter. But before that, let me mention what comes to mind: it is not uncommon for us to blame others for our own troubles and afflictions that originate from sources other than those we attribute them to. As Valerius Martial said: "Under a harsh ruler, and in times of adversity, you dared to be good."

Doesn't the most ignorant person realize how much influence the times and public affairs have on the minds of private citizens? It is possible that you encounter extremely corrupt customs and ways of living full of pretence and falsehood. Have you ever considered if there is any place on earth where, as the number of people increases, so do the traps, deceitful words, lies, and perjury? It is inevitable to be influenced by such people in public life. And you, Nicola, know very well how much power fortune has over us mortals, or rather, how much power we mortals have over fortune. You, Battista, recognize our times and how many good people lead miserable lives that are unworthy of their virtues. Conversely, observe the monstrosities and unimaginable things that have arisen due to fortune. As the satirical poet Juvenal said: "If Fortune wills it, you will become consul instead of an orator; If she wills it the other way, you will become an orator instead of consul."

And if it is true that the heavens have considerable influence over us, it is our task to act like a gambler: if luck is on our side, we win; if we encounter unfavourable circumstances, we moderate them according to the best reasoning available. And certainly, as the excellent ancient proverb says, we must live today as we live today. It is said that sound advice and self-control are the keys to a happy life. Yes, but what if someone considers themselves well-advised simply because they refuse to endure what is necessary due to their circumstances and fortunes? Thales of Miletus said that necessity conquers. And what can bring about a necessity equal to that of the heavens? Therefore, as the poet Manilius rightly said: "Alas, it is not right for anyone to trust unwilling gods."

And indeed, consider Virgil's priest Laocoon, who, while seeking the welfare of his homeland, struck the wooden horse, dedicated to Pallas and filled with armed warriors, with a spear. It was a fatal time during the fall of Troy, and he was not believed. I don't want to make a mistake by attributing an inevitable necessity from the heavens to all human affairs, which I completely deny. Perhaps, just as doctors administer treatments to the sick that would be harmful to the healthy and, at times, indulge in charms and superstitions themselves when they are in pain, we, in our disturbances and weak state of mind, will listen to someone who may have said that what is happening now could not have been otherwise and that certain conditions and causes, perhaps harmonious and fateful, made it inevitable. And once certain events have occurred, they will last only as long as the celestial and fateful forces that govern them permit, as they are ever-changing and unstable. Therefore, things will neither remain constant nor endure in a fixed state. As Propertius said: "Times change; certainly, loves change. And even the gods themselves, and harsh days, change."

We see the same volatility in public affairs as in private matters. The Roman Republic did not always enjoy success and victory; they encountered the formidable Hannibal, who inflicted significant losses upon them. Likewise, Hannibal did not always have favourable fortune against the Romans; he was defeated by Marcellus, proving that Carthaginian armies could be overcome. Therefore, we should approach fortune like Demofon, as described by

Diogenes Laërtius, who sought shade from the sun and sweated in the shade. When times and events appear challenging, we must rely on counsel and prudence to navigate through adversity. And where misfortune seems unavoidable, we must summon the strength of character to endure it. We should not be like those weakened individuals who, at the slightest sign of adversity, fall into sadness, languish, and give up hope. Let us condemn the Gallograeci mentioned by Justinus, who, fearing an imminent unfortunate outcome in their sacrifices, cowardly killed their mothers and children, lost everything, burned their homes and possessions, and themselves. It was an immense frenzy, harming themselves out of fear of harm. Many situations, initiated by their very beginnings, seem harsh and detrimental but eventually turn out contrary to our expectations, resulting in a positive outcome and benefit. In this regard, I find your Apologue 88, Battista, quite fitting, where lakes believed that clouds were mountains suspended in the air above them, ready to fall upon their heads. Consequently, the lakes became pale, gloomy, and trembled. However, when they saw those clouds dissolve into rain and water, they all rejoiced and exuded happiness. As the saying goes in Terence's Eunuchus, sometimes misfortune tends to bring about great good. It has happened to many others, including that Jason from Phaedrus, who, receiving a wound from his enemies, was subsequently cured of an ailment that had previously been incurable by medical treatment due to the incision made by his adversaries. Therefore, let us confront anticipated troubles with counsel and reason to avoid them or to prepare ourselves to endure them well. First and foremost, it is beneficial to foster positive expectations about forthcoming events. Even if things turn out unfavourably, at least you will live without the anxiety and distress that accompany worry. Similarly, when times appear joyful, introduce a measure of caution as if tempering excessive elation. And if any unforeseen obstacle hinders your just and commendable endeavours, do not abandon yourself. Do as the Sibyl advised Aeneas:

"Do not yield to misfortunes, but advance more boldly against them than your fortune will allow you. The path to salvation, which you least expect, will be revealed from the Greek city."

It is said that nothing is a more reliable provider than the earth. It fulfills what you entrust to it, not just equally but in greater measure, as prescribed by Hesiod. You will find even greater faithfulness in your industry and diligence, especially when directed towards honorable and worthy endeavors, as the heavens and fate themselves conspire to reward your merits. Virtue has never been without the reward of praise and favor. Allow me to present this argument: the affairs of this world are governed either by us humans or by others like us, mortal beings. If others govern them, let us entrust the responsibility to those who have already managed them for countless years with reason and goodness. But if, as you write in one of your delightful intercenals, Battista, the fortunes of mortal beings do not come from the heavens but are born out of the foolishness of people, then let them be shaped by humans such as yourself, inclined and subject to every passion and fickleness of the soul. Your opinion pleases me, and I confirm it. For if Caesar had not elevated Octavian to such greatness, and if his comrades had not submitted to Caesar, neither of them would have become rulers and ministers of such an empire. Perhaps one would have remained a silversmith, similar to his father, and the other perhaps a lawyer. Therefore, if things in our lives unfold against our will, they happen according to the will of those who guide them in such a way. It would indeed be insufferable arrogance on my part to desire that everything should bend to my own will and nothing should deviate from my plans and intentions. We fulfill so many of our desires elsewhere; now let others find satisfaction in some of their own wishes. But now that we have arrived at this most sacred temple, let us enter to pay homage to the name and image of God. And what helps us the most, beyond all the teachings and warnings of the wisest writers, is to pray that God does not impose harsh conditions upon us, but grants us good mental health, sound counsel, unwavering physical strength, and a courageous and steadfast spirit to endure and withstand the onslaught and burdens of adverse circumstances.

BOOK III

In the two previous books, we explored various useful remedies to avoid being disturbed. You saw several specific and concise remedies to calm the negative movements of the soul when they arise in us due to our own mistakes, the vices of others, or the changing times, the fickleness of fortune, and the hardships of our circumstances. Now, there remain certain general admonitions suited to purging any deep-seated and stubborn melancholy within us—an undoubtedly valuable and worthy subject that will be discussed in this third book by our Agnolo and our Niccola, highly civilized and knowledgeable men. Perhaps not with the level of dignity befitting their authority and excellence, for I confess that I lack such eloquence and genius to emulate the gravity and maturity of Agnolo Pandolfini in my writings, and I affirm that I cannot express the subtlety of intellect and quickness of understanding that I know Niccola possesses. Nor do I feel sufficiently practiced to artfully and orderly combine and conclude such exquisite doctrine and marvellous erudition as each of our citizens senses and has long known to exist in both of them. However, the arguments they present will be so self-evidently excellent that I have no doubt you will delight in recognizing their merit, regardless of my eloquence and ability to convey them. Listen to them, as you have done so far, with eagerness and attentiveness, and imagine yourself as a fourth participant in these discussions led by our Agnolo, a truly upright and wise man. As for the recent debates, when we left the church and took a few steps, he stopped and, taking hold of Niccola and me by the hand, he shook his head slightly and said, "I thought I had fully planned and concluded this endeavour, and I believed that nothing remained in this matter but the final conclusion and brief enumeration of the things we presented. But now I realize my mistake in several ways, and I wish I had not started something that I did not know how to lead in an organized manner up to this point. Nor do I know where to direct it now, as I see from afar that it should be guided elsewhere. I have said many things, and perhaps they were not useless, but it happened to me as if I found the top of a large rock in the vineyard and thought it should be uncovered, but then I regretted the sweat and time I wasted on it until now, where I see it is larger and more difficult to move and transport than I anticipated."

Thus spoke Agnolo, and then he fell silent again and resumed walking. Then Niccola, a very astute man, slowed down and said to me, "Shall we agree, Battista, with Agnolo's statement that his previous arguments were without order? And shall we say that the abundance of various, highly worthy, and extremely rare things collected by him were not presented in a place and arrangement befitting their beauty? Many of our esteemed Latin predecessors, as well as many Greeks, Agnolo, wrote similar parts and sections of philosophy. However, I have never seen anyone among them, including you, compose and arrange them more meticulously than you did. I noticed in every argument and progression of your discourse an incredible brevity combined with a marvellous abundance and fullness of weighty and fitting sayings and sentences. What I find praiseworthy in someone who writes or, as you do here, discusses and reasons about these doctrines pertaining to virtue and living well and happily, Agnolo, is precisely what initially struck me as beautiful in you. I don't know if it was Cypresses, who Vitruvius praises so highly, or another architect who invented this style of painting and depicting the floor as they do today. But whoever it was, the creator of such a charming thing, perhaps adorned the most splendid temple of Ephesus, which all of Asia constructed in no less than seven hundred years. This person saw the massive walls of the building piled up and enhanced with huge sections of marble from the mountains. They saw towering columns on all sides, as well as bronze-covered beams and the roof adorned with gold. Inside and outside, they observed grand slabs of porphyry and jasper arranged and applied in distinct patterns, and everything appeared splendid. They marvelled at every part, which was adorned and filled with wonders, except that the floor remained bare and neglected. Thus, to adorn and diversify the floor, distinct from the rest of the temple, this person took the remaining small scraps of marble, porphyry, and jasper from the entire structure and combined them together, arranging them according to their colours and shapes, thereby clothing and beautifying the entire floor. This work was no less pleasing and enjoyable than the grandest parts of the rest of the building. The same happens with scholars. The intellects of Asia, especially the Greeks, were inventors of all arts and disciplines over many years. Together, they constructed an almost temple-like dwelling in their writings for Athena and Pronea, the goddess of Stoic philosophers. They expanded the walls through the exploration of truth and falsehood. They established columns by discerning and recording the effects and forces of nature. They added a roof that would protect such a work from adverse storms. This expertise involved avoiding evil, pursuing and attaining good, abhorring vice, seeking and loving virtue. But what happens? The opposite of what occurred above. That person collected the remaining fragments and composed the floor. However, where I, like that person, and like the other, wanted to adorn my small and private space, I took from that public and noble building what seemed suitable for my own designs, and I divided it into several parts, distributing them wherever I saw fit. And from this came, as they say, "Nothing new under the sun." These literary elements are seen taken by so many and used and spread in their writings, that now for anyone who wants to discuss them, there is nothing left but to gather and arrange them and then combine them together with some variety from others and suitability to their own work, as if their purpose were to imitate in this the one who made the floor elsewhere.

What I delight in and consider as the ultimate achievement is when I see things combined together in such a way that they harmonize with their prescribed colours in a specific and designated form and painting, and where I see no serious gaps or unsightly voids among them. Who could be so fastidious as to not approve and praise the person who, with such great skill and diligence, created such a harmonious work? And we, Agnolo, who see gathered by you what was scattered and worn out among all other writers, and we hear so many diverse things brought together, compacted, embedded, and interwoven, all in perfect harmony, all equal on the same level, all following the same pattern, not only do we no longer desire anything more here, nor do we merely approve and praise it, but we are also deeply grateful and acknowledge your merit. Furthermore, it was not only the rare and marvellous weaving and knotting together of various sayings and weighty maxims that impressed us, but it was primarily the almost divine conception and description of the entire subject matter presented by you. You comprehended a matter that none of the ancient masters had touched upon before, and you showed how to ward off and exclude melancholy. And in each subsequent step of your reasoning, I confess, you delighted me greatly and kept me continuously engaged and attentive, and your every word strongly convinced me. I am reminded of the story they tell about Alexander the Great, who, when presented with a beautifully crafted small box, did not know what to place inside it, something precious and worthy of being housed in such a marvellous case. Therefore, he ordered that the books of Homer be placed and kept inside it, which certainly, I do not deny, are a true mirror of human life.

But what did Homer intend by depicting such unheard-of and stubborn patience in his Ulysses? If patience is what makes us indifferent to offenses, wouldn't it be more praiseworthy to disregard them entirely and leave to others not only the judgment and decision but also the effort of punishing and, by punishing, making those who have treated you poorly better? And if patience in us means pretending not to feel what burdens us, then I am not the one who approves and prefers this approach of seeking revenge in life, enduring more and more torment for the sake of avenging an insult, at the expense of myself and my dignity. I have never been able to adapt myself to not caring and tolerating the audacity and insolence of others without considering it a sign of servility and worthy of reproach. They praise this trait and place it above the highest virtues, claiming that patience, coupled with courteous behaviour, triumphs over armed Furies. If enduring constant annoyances and being weighed down by the gravest and intolerable troubles is victory, then they speak the truth. I see and experience this in myself every day, that my suffering brings me nothing but insults. Enduring only opens the way for others' insolence to grow and become more burdensome to you. Enduring from hour to hour exposes you to new obstacles and harsh offenses. Enduring has never been beneficial except insofar as it demonstrates that one is both free and a dangerous person. And as for how unpleasant, burdensome, difficult, and tedious it is to tolerate the foolishness of others, that is a matter for another discussion. But does it truly help, in living and interacting with the multitude, to conceal our own desires and neglect ourselves, disregarding our own dignity, which you call patience? Tell me, what virtue will relieve us when we are oppressed by adverse circumstances and the ruins of our times? The wise will say: Do not care about your pains. Easy to say, easy to say. But how will someone who has lost their personal possessions, family, relatives, friends, and all their comforts and honours, who has lost their domestic wealth, rank, public authority, and place of dignity, and now finds themselves in solitude, besieged by every necessity, abject, deprived, and perhaps weak and infirm in their nerves and limbs, how will they sustain themselves? Perhaps you will bring up those very common and well-known sayings: "Don't be upset about your blindness, don't be burdened by your deafness." When you can no longer see or hear many things that used to cause you distress, you still see quite clearly when you can distinguish between good and bad things, between worthy and unworthy things, and you still hear quite well when you hear yourself in those things that contribute to virtue and praise. And the night still holds its own delights. Fortunes, fame, status, the happiness of life—will you say that these are transient and fragile things? Yet they are the very things for which all mortals contend with swords and fire, for which they expend their sweat, blood, and lives. And you expect me not to care for them or desire them? And yet, Agnolo, it pains me, and I am pained by not having them. And even though I prepare my mind and firmly resolve not to care or desire what is forbidden and lost to me, still, when I often see places and things, when I hear and perceive this and that, when my thoughts wander from one thing to another, then, not only as Dido said near Virgil: "I recognize the traces of the ancient flame," but even before that, my sad memories are renewed, my sorrows are reignited, and I also say: "Sweet mementos, as long as fate and the gods allowed."

"And tears come to me before I realize it, whether it be due to error or sorrow. You might ask, 'Why do you cry?' I would respond as the philosopher Solon did: 'I cry because I feel that crying brings no relief to my sorrow.' But who would reproach me for this? We see even wild animals around their nests and dens openly display signs of their distress. And wise was the saying of Nestor's son, as recorded by our Homer: 'I do not praise weeping.' I consider it no shame to weep for one's dead, for this is the only honour that should be given to miserable mortals who have passed away. Look at King Priam, the most prudent ruler, who commanded that for nine full days there should be mourning for his mighty son Hector, and on the tenth day he should be buried and funeral rites performed, and on the eleventh day he ordered the construction of the most honourable tomb. In these funeral ceremonies, there were those who, through mournful expressions, songs, and verses, incited sadness and sighs in those who heard and saw. Similarly, we praise Marcus Fabius, who, upon losing his brother, declined the laurel wreath, a distinguished public honour. But why do we recount examples of mortal rulers, when we can better understand what is approved in this regard by learned

and renowned writers, such as when the goddess
among gods, as described by Homer, took the black
veil in her mourning and sorrow?"

AGNOLO: Now, Niccolo, as a man who has always
been more patient than others throughout your life,
continue to argue and dissuade patience with me.
If I wanted to show you how wisdom, as they say,
avoids the foolishness of the common people and
refrains from yielding to the tempests of popular
opinion, it has always been the most beneficial course
of action. And if I wanted to explain to you how
being measured, deliberate, and not hasty in one's
thoughts and actions is necessary for a virtuous life,
conducive to goodness and happiness, allowing one
to lead a life full of purpose, full of achievements,
full of merit, and devoid of difficulties, displeasures,
or inconveniences for those who are guided by
reason, well-established in virtue, and seek to earn
praise and good reputation among mortals and
future generations, a single day would not be enough.
I would be inundated with a wealth of excellent
arguments. Perhaps we can discuss this further at
another time according to your preference. For now,
as it pertains to our topic, I will not be displeased if
you offer advice based on the necessities and timing
of your own circumstances. What do you say? I am
troubled by offenses. I desire valuable things. So,
what shall we do? At the first provocation, we will
resist and defend ourselves. Look, Niccolo, at how
useful this advice is. You may say, "And what do you
think, Agnolo?" You see how willingly and openly
I engage with you. I would rather not be heard by

these philosophers of mine. I say, Niccolo, and you, Battista, that in enduring, one should either have nothing or have too much. In other matters, moderation is useful. But in this case, where you cannot present yourself freely, obey those with more power. To the poet Euripides, the disobedience of the masses seemed more destructive than fire and more capable of consuming things. They say that the multitude has always been unconquerable. Homer said that evil always prevails, but necessity will teach you when, where, and to whom you should yield. Consider it necessary to yield whenever yielding does not worsen your situation, and regard any change that, for now, can only be for the better as excellent. In all other respects, I agree that when it is permissible for you, show yourself as a man with some spirit. Suppress and lessen the arrogance that ignites your anger.

So, I will not be displeased if you advise me according to the necessities and opportunities of your own time in every endeavour and matter. I do not distract you from your human senses and inclinations, nor do I forbid you from feeling the pain of losing things dear and beloved to you. However, I remind you not to persist in sorrow, nor should you continue to find it burdensome and unproductive for yourself and your needs. You desire and seek what mortals value and prioritize, for which they exert sweat, blood, and even their lives. If it is possible to acquire and regain these things through grieving and weeping, as many do, then go ahead; live in constant and profound sorrow until you are satisfied and fulfil your desires and expectations. Do as Marcus Livius, a highly respected man in Rome, did. He hoped for and promised himself the consulship, but when he was rejected by the people and his expectations were shattered during his pursuit of the consulship, he considered it a disgrace. As a result, he secluded himself, avoiding public squares, theatres, temples, and any prominent place. He even fled his homeland and spent eight years in a sorrowful and wretched life in the countryside. And if you find that your lamentation, your mourning within yourself, and your living in sadness and grief bring you nothing of the many things you desire, what foolishness would it be not to relinquish what torments and crushes you? Nothing burdens our souls as much as being saddened by other disturbances. Lust carries a certain heat, immoderate joy carries an inept levity, and fear carries a sense of mistrust and excessive humility. But this state of mind they call sadness, this lamentation and living tediously within oneself, contains greater inherent and entrenched evils. Homer said that misery quickly ages us. And you can see how the sorrowful become deformed, languid, and utterly consumed by their inner torments, much like a decaying beam plagued by woodworms, rotting and becoming filthy. So what madness is it to continue nurturing within yourself what seduces and separates you from all your hope and expectation? Why do you persist where grieving and sadness bring no benefit but much harm? Don't you realize that immersing and pushing yourself with thoughts into this thicket of your sad and ungrateful memories renders you incapable of discerning and distinguishing what aligns with your well-being in life? It makes you useless in devising and planning good, opportune, and effective strategies to avoid and overcome the dangers and difficulties that constantly arise and confront us from many sides in life. If your troubles cause you pain, you are the one to blame by indulging in ineffective self-pity. If you mourn the loss of your pleasures, acknowledge your fault and escape from all sorrow. Seek new delights, joys, and pleasures elsewhere.

If the loss of your integrity and position disturbs you, you are remaining in a state of self-deception. You fail to recognize that, by your own prudence, you should have already realized that you are not so different from other mortals. You should acknowledge and accept that you are subject to the various chances and fickleness of fortune. What justice would it be if you obstinately refuse to acknowledge any of the conditions that come with life? What prudence is it to not recognize yourself as a human being? What modesty is it to not put an end to your complaints, no matter the circumstances? What praise of great and steadfast character would it be if you, who were born to rule and govern others, cannot control yourself? And if moderation, reason, and virtue are necessary in certain matters, they are certainly needed when it comes to pain. Orestes became furious due to sorrow. Cleobulus, a philosopher, ended his life due to his heavy melancholy. Echo suggests that she turned into a dog and went mad because of the intense pangs of her sorrows. They say Niobe transformed into stone from the unbearable anguish. Therefore, since pain can turn a person into a raging beast, a mad creature, or an insensible rock, why wouldn't you make every effort to distance yourself from this lamentation? But, Niccola, in all my arguments, you see that I do not forbid you from being a man of your own opinions and will, but I do forbid you from becoming cruel and inhuman. Yet, you still cling to it, like a trapped quail in a cage that desires to escape even for a little space that seems unsatisfactory to it. Perhaps you wish to engage in further debate and expand your arguments against mine. Oh, how oppressive and powerful pain is! It prevails. It is difficult and challenging not to feel and yield to its miseries. In the tragedy written by Aeschylus, when he presents the gods who come to console Prometheus, relegated and bound to that rock in the Caucasus, they do not say, "Prometheus, do not care about your suffering and do not feel it." Instead, they say, "What is imposed on you by the supreme Zeus, what you cannot refuse, what is necessary for you to endure, bear it with as little agitation and fury as possible." Yet, Prometheus still complains with immoderate words, saying, "I caused mortals to never die again. I gave them much blind hope and added that living, celestial fire." And there, Oceanus, the greatest of the gods, responds, "Prometheus, abandon your ancient arrogance and boasting. Adopt new customs when the heavens serve new tyrants, and temper your language and insolence altogether. The anger of those who have power over you will be appeased more by your submission than by your arrogance. The anger that burns you can be extinguished and healed with humble words. It would benefit you to appear less wise and less learned than we are. The Fates, the triform sisters, and the ever-remembering Furies are ministers of Necessity."

Thus spoke Oceanus to Prometheus. And in the works of Euripides, a Greek poet and tragedian, Ulysses said to Hecuba when he announced that the Greek army deemed it necessary for the well-being and honour of Greece to sacrifice his daughter to the gods: "Consider, Hecuba, your misfortunes are no longer distant, and without defiance, give what you cannot deny to your circumstances." It has always been the wise thing to use wisdom even in unfavourable situations. And what will we do in our adversities? Will we not heed these excellent admonitions worthy of being sent and observed for perpetual remembrance? Instead, like wild colts, we will fight and exhaust ourselves, resisting and struggling against those who try to guide and restrain us? Will we not be softened or supported by those who hold us bound and curb our actions? And how will we regard someone who, disposed to desire what is irrecoverable, becomes more burdened with worries from the smallest sparks of their extinguished memories, oblivious to their error except through their own tears? Why do you weep, effeminate man? I have lost; I have nothing; I desire. These spoilt children learn to cry from their mother's excessive indulgence, and when they don't receive what they ask for, they find solace in weeping. And we, in this matter, are even more delicate and less sensible than infants, as we persist in writhing and sobbing in our self-pity, knowing well that it is of no avail. When many gods gathered at Phoebus' house to comfort him in the case of his son Phaeton, Phoebus pleased them by inviting them and preparing the customary feast and reclining banquet. Among those deities were Tears and Laughter, twin brothers born from the goddess Mollizie and that Faun known as Stolidasperum. Pirtheus, the organizer of the event, proceeded to arrange seats and places for the guests. When he came to these two brothers, he paused, astonished by how alike they were in every aspect and feature; he could hardly discern any distinguishing mark that would differentiate one from the other, as both had distorted faces unlike the other gods. Their mouths were inverted, their brows contracted and knotted, their eyes watery and dim, their hands, chests, and shoulders entangled and disjointed. Only one difference stood out: one of them appeared entirely covered in drool and filth, while the other was not as dirty and disagreeable to look at. Pirtheus marvelled and said, "I cannot decide who should sit before the other; but whichever one of you moves first, the other shall follow."

And these two remained almost dumbfounded, not speaking but breaking out into the most obscene and indecent sounds and gestures. Pirtheus, seeing them in such obscene and transformed states, marvelled that among the ranks of the greatest and noblest gods, there were two such obscene and disagreeable monsters. And in his astonishment, as he stared at them intently, he noticed that one of them feigned a similar expression of astonishment on his own face, mirroring the gaze and mental state of the other. Whatever one of them contorted, the other imitated in the same way. Some of the gods laughed at their foolishness, while others perhaps sympathized with their great misfit, and they excluded them, saying, "You have neither the face to honour such a gathering, nor the countenance to console the unfortunate." Indeed, if one were to see oneself when crying, they would either mock such faint-heartedness or be repulsed by their own ugliness. You may ask: Who can hold back tears in their times of suffering? It is a natural inclination. Even animals in the forests and deserts give clear signs of their distress. Perhaps, just as in many other things, and in this case as well, they are still animals, desiring what they cannot find, or believing that through their cries and frenzy, they may more quickly and effortlessly obtain what they may be pursuing. And you, human, why do you weep? If you had something else to do, surely you would not be weeping. During the final destruction of Jerusalem, when more than six hundred thousand known Jews perished from famine, they not only did not weep but also neglected to bury their loved ones. Ulysses, in Homer's account—our esteemed Homer, whom I often mention with delight, as he may also be a mirror of human life to you—requested, during a meal, that his audience allow him to satisfy his hunger and thirst before he recounted his own experiences, as hunger makes me forget all other concerns. And Ulysses' companions did not begin to weep for their lost loved ones until after the meal on the island of

Hyperion. Whom will you find that does not have an abundance of greater and more necessary, useful, and worthy matters than weeping? And if this madness of weeping pleases you, at least let it be accompanied by some justification.

Let us leave behind other matters that have been clearly and plainly expressed, which, whenever it may be, would dignify our tears. Who ever weeps for just one of the many wasted or misused days of their life? And what do you think is worse: losing something that can never be regained or restored, or losing things that are meant to be lost and capable of being recovered? I don't want to elaborate or embellish this point. I simply say that if we, as educated individuals, are permitted to weep, it should be when we waste time or make a mistake. But even here, I don't want to be too strict or austere with you. Just as in battle, the strongest soldier, when feeling exhausted and overwhelmed, allows themselves to yield somewhat to their comrades, but not among the most experienced troops, and there they wipe away the sweat and remove the blood from the wound received in a vulnerable spot where they were not properly protected. And I won't blame you if you shed a few tears in accordance with the customs and expectations of others, as a sign and testimony of your humanity. But in this matter, listen to your Homer, where Ulysses says: "We must control our tears, so that no woman sees us with wet faces and thinks we might be drunk." It is certainly far removed from any manly steadfastness to present oneself as either resembling a woman or someone lacking sobriety and self-control. It is our duty as men to do no more than what Aeneas did near Virgil, who, amidst countless dangers and surrounding hardships, only sighed and raised his hands to the stars. The abundance of tears, bitter cries, feminine wails, and shrieks are unworthy of a man. Among the Liti, a highly civilized people, there was a law that anyone who wished to cry should dress in women's clothing. But if, even amidst those manly groans, you happen to add a tear or two and release an intimate sigh, do so in moderation. Numa, the king of the Romans, a highly religious and pious man, forbade mourning for the dead for more months than the number of years the deceased had lived; and he did not want children under the age of three to be mourned at all. After the devastating defeat at Cannae, the Roman Senate, deeply affected for the rest of their lives, commanded an end to mourning in Rome, and their weeping was not to extend beyond the thirtieth day. On the third day, Caesar the dictator put an end to all domestic and public mourning by dignifying and honouring the funeral of his deceased daughter. So, as soon as we can, let us put an end to these utterly useless follies.

Nor does the feminine lightness of weeping and tearing one's cheeks or pulling out one's hair bother me as much as the madness of many who, in their self-conceived melancholy, lose sleep, abandon food, lose themselves, avoid seeing and being seen by other people, and in their solitude and shadow, remain foolish and almost numb. They lament and preach about being the most miserable and unfortunate of all mortals, yet they continue to add to their own unhappiness and misery by brooding and tormenting themselves with sad memories and conceived resentments and displeasures.

But we are extremely imprudent when we fail to understand our own state. If, as Socrates said, we were to gather all our misfortunes together, each person would find their own ancient burdens to be lighter than taking on this new, unprecedented weight and distress that would befall them if the total sum of all the universal woes of mortals were evenly distributed by fate. And how much more bearable would Priam's fate be, of whom those verses sing, too tender and greatly poignant, to incite compassion for the misfortunes of others and to restrain us from impulsive actions and immoderate desires:

"This is the end of Priam's destiny; this is how fate, by chance, led him to witness Troy in flames and fallen Pergamum, once proud ruler of many peoples and lands of Asia..."

I won't go into detail about his calamities. How fortunate he would be if he had not been assigned more than his share of that total sum Socrates mentioned, imposed upon him by his own fortune.

Next... it was a custom that the sick would lie outside the vestibules and entrances of the temple. Those who entered to greet God would see and hear every progression of their illness and say, "The same thing happened to so-and-so, and it happened to me too. We tried this and that remedy, and we were healed." It seems to me that our practice is the opposite, where the doctors, from whom we learn how to heal ourselves, stand at the vestibules of our temples. How much relief, Niccola, these afflicted and weary ones, naked, wounded, in old age, extremely weak, sitting and lying where you place your feet, bring to me as they beg for alms and pity. Then, Battista, then we will take excellent and healing remedies. He is poor and asks me for help; I am rich and give. He has every limb exposed; I, even down to my hands and much of my face (parts that should be well-covered), keep them clothed and protected. He is covered in scabs, leprosy, filthiness, burdened with diseases and covered in foul and infectious fluids; I am clean, splendid, and entirely charming. If everything were distributed by chance, I would have a share of such obscenity and filthiness; and even though it isn't distributed that way, I am still far happier than he is. Oh, he is lazy, careless, and enjoys being no one other than himself; yet he is covered in the same filth as you. It should move you to pity him all the more, and at the same time, it should make you recognize your own fortune and his calamity, especially considering that his limbs and mind are less healthy than yours. Now tell me, that noble Mecenas of old, born of noble ancestors, that friend and patron of all good scholars, did he seem worthy of constant affliction due to his nobility? He endured a perpetual fever throughout most of his life, without even a brief moment of sleep. It would be far too divine a thing not to be careless, if only that generation of men were to suffer the ultimate miseries.

But I won't dwell on it, as recounting the miseries of mortals would take up the whole day. What I'm saying is that not only recognizing ourselves as human beings and contemplating the fate and condition of humanity, as we discussed yesterday, helps alleviate melancholy, but it also aids in purging the miseries that have already taken root within our souls. It's not just recognizing yourself, but also anything that drives away and removes disturbances from us; it also cleanses and restores our already contaminated and corrupted souls. And especially those arguments you would use to console others will bring great benefit to yourself. Perhaps these will be such arguments: if one of the mortals was the one who wronged you—wrong is a bad thing because there was never a wrong without vice, nor vice without fault—but the vice and the wrong remain with him, not with you, but with the one who committed it. If the harm is someone else's, you shouldn't be distressed by it. And if perhaps it was the heavens and those ministers of God's will, whom the ancient theologians called gods, who brought you into calamity, accept it in a better light, for you have received so many blessings from them, which by their nature have always been beneficial, generous, and desirous of seeing you better. Add to that it has always been the duty of the wise to provide for themselves so that nothing oppresses them. Similarly, it has always been the duty of a strong soul to endure whatever adversity may come. In your misfortunes, I want you to seek help from God. But I don't want you to abandon yourself and believe that you cannot do for yourself what you can.

Remain, whenever it may be, beseeching the gods with your prayers and requests. Stir up your virtue within you: Let a sound mind be in a sound body. Our mind will be sound as much as we want it to be. We can certainly seek good fortune from the gods. But we must seek virtue from ourselves; through our own efforts, our own diligence, we will obtain wisdom, the adornments of the soul, and praise for a well-composed mind. Perhaps you seek wisdom and virtue from the gods in your adverse circumstances, and immediately prudence will present itself to you, advising you to persist in your lamenting, which will bring you no benefit. And along with prudence, there comes temperance, which disapproves of any immoderate and immature action or speech. And first of all, justice, the light and splendour of all virtues, accuses and accuses you, where you deviate from manliness and the just and upright state of living, abandoning yourself and your duty. And fortitude, which is disgusted by any weakness of yours and despises anything that is not excellent and lofty. How well will you be received while you lie in solitude and darkness, wasting away? So, comfort yourself now, help yourself, prepare yourself to conquer, and you will conquer through your virtue whenever you wish, and you will even surprise yourself by conquering those whom you least expect. This adverse fortune of yours will teach you to be patient; patience will strengthen your manliness, and with manliness, one conquers, and by conquering in every battle, one becomes strongest and unbeatable.

Fortune, on its own, rest assured, has always been and will always be extremely weak and feeble against those who oppose it. But you, don't add to the leftovers and reluctance of fortune the sinister impulses from within yourself. Even though you go against yourself and your laziness, and against any necessary tranquillity of your soul, avoid fighting against yourself and instead focus your efforts where you feel the weakest and least prepared and armed. In every thought you have within yourself, avoid indulging in self-pity, every gesture, and every self-gratification that you wouldn't display in the presence of friends and enemies. Just as an anchor secures itself in the sea, anchor and affirm yourself with sound reason and manliness in every tumult of your emotions and mind. And it will greatly benefit you to console yourself with some joyful memories of the past or pleasant expectations of things to come, contrasting your misfortunes with the blessings and praise that have come to you from your fortunes, your physical well-being, or your intellectual achievements. And it will benefit you to do as Aeneas did in his difficult circumstances and trials: "I bear in mind the past and pay for it with the fate of my future." For such anticipated blessings, not injuries, are the reasons behind these and greater hardships. The fewer people there are who could endure these difficulties with an unbroken and equable spirit, the greater will be my praise for having endured them. And how beautifully Virgil, the great poet, settled this reasoning in several places as a way to console himself in his afflicted and sorrowful state. Here are verses by Battista in his Tuscan poems, in which he imitated Virgil: "We have suffered more grievous things elsewhere, and time will bring an end to these as well." And Aeneas, close to Virgil, said: "Perhaps one day, it will be pleasing to remember even these things." In her final fury and extreme cruelty, Dido, before her hasty death, could not console herself otherwise: "I built a glorious city, I saw my own walls."

After Homer, when Hector was mortally wounded, he comforted himself by hoping for immortal glory and eternal fame. He said, "I have fulfilled my destiny. I may leave this life prematurely, but I do not leave without having achieved some full and well-earned glory, when I did many things worthy of remembrance and posterity." And Ulysses, who endured many insults from King Alcinous of the Phaeacians, when he saw that the gods were reconciled with him, and the winds favoured his journey at sea, forgot all past adversities and found great consolation in the presence of every good thing.

Likewise, it would be appropriate for us to discipline ourselves with just admonitions, strengthen ourselves with true and complete reasons, and console ourselves with hope, pleasant memories, and joyful contentment of the mind. But we, being lazy and idle, despite the many reasons and admonitions presented by me until now, and the many ways to seek revenge in freedom and liberate ourselves from our most ungrateful troubles, perhaps don't find them suitable. Instead, we lie down and groan, desiring someone with their own skill and without any effort or diligence on our part to restore us to integrity and a stable state of mind. We wish to have here among us that Peion, the physician of the gods, who never leaves the presence of Jupiter and constantly assists him at dinner. Although I'm not sure if he could do for us what we cannot do for ourselves, unless that Helen, daughter of Jupiter, as described by Homer, offered him that potion with which she induced forgetfulness of all sorrows to anyone who drank it. That would be a useful thing for us mortals. Although Diodorus, the Greek historian, mentions a certain kind of medicine called "elena," composed by the wife of Tono the physician, which extinguishes tears and banishes sorrow. But let me laugh with you, Niccolo; however, I will not say something that is not relevant to these discussions, when it is said that there is no one among the gods, who are the ministers of nature and the compensators of human condition, who can provide a remedy for our mental ailments through intellect, ointments, or medicines. Let's turn to any help and support that may alleviate our weakness and affliction from oppressive burdens. I laugh. They say that Bacchus, among the number of the gods, was called Liber Pater, since he liberated the soul from worries, soothed pain, and made it rejuvenated. And he achieved this only through wine, the lively and joyful fruit of the earth. Many accuse Flaccus, the lyric poet, falsely attributing to all of us elderly people, and accuse him of being a drinker because he praises wine in many of his odes. Certainly, as they say about us old and exhausted people, "senectus aquilae" (the old age of an eagle).

Therefore, I do not want to appear in my words less sober than I have always been throughout my life. In this case, I want to prejudge and predetermine that I condemn the immodesty of wine in every other aspect of life. I have seen and noted in many other places strong and vibrant men whose intemperance in wine brought them down and shortened their lives, depriving them of good health. I will not go into detail about how being not sober enough burdens our bodies with severe illnesses. But Homer calls sleep the conqueror of all bitterness, and he tells how Athena, the goddess who always supported Ulysses in every adversity, approached him after his miserable shipwreck when he reached the shore on the third day. Moved by pity, the goddess Athena, unlike in his shipwreck, did not provide him with a veil or garment on which he could rest his chest and limbs. Instead, she simply induced sleep upon him, to temporarily free him from his many miseries, and he fell asleep. A similar story is told about Stratonice near Iesippus in history. She was captured by victorious enemies and decided to escape servitude and kill herself. But just as she was seeking ways to satisfy herself with less pain and more dignity, she was interrupted and overtaken by sleep. She slept, and in that sleep, her fury and cruelty were extinguished.

Therefore, they say that sleep is a sweet forgetfulness of all troubles. And, if I may add, Niccola, wine seems to be an excellent inducer of sleep. Following the advice of Diomedes: eat and drink well, then you will find solace in sleep. Although in our comedy,

Cherea says in his amorous exploits: "I will tire myself out on the estate by doing some work, so that I can sleep soundly afterwards." Homer found new remedies for this, where he introduces Thetis, who suggests to her sorrowful son something which I won't mention, as you know she says: "My son, find pleasure with a tender maiden tonight." And elsewhere your esteemed Homer states that sexual intercourse brings about a sweet and harmless sleep. The Greeks call the troubles of the soul "acidos." Hence, they named Venus "acidalia," as she alleviates the sorrows of the soul. But what shall we say about wine? Recall how many times it is used to alleviate the heavy burdens of the soul. Juno complained that she was not as accepted by Jupiter as she desired, and Vulcan, the cupbearer of the gods, gave her wine with which she could wash away all sadness. And Laodice, the wife of Elicanor, gave sweet wine to her weary son involved in warfare, and said: "Drinking restores strength and fortifies the soul." Historian Julius writes that Maximinus, one of the successors to Caesar and the ruler of the Roman Empire, used to consume forty pounds of meat in one day and drink an amphora of wine. He used to collect his own sweat when he exerted himself and often showed three jars filled with his sweat. This man, considered an enemy of the state by the Senate, was so enraged that he struck his head against a wall in fury and attempted to gouge out his son's eye. Only one excellent remedy helped in such a state of frenzy: getting drunk. And although I dare not criticize this remedy, which indeed helps, it is not something I find appealing. Many things done may please us at the moment but are not beautiful in themselves.

And I also see that this use of wine did not displease many excellent and worthy men. Solon and Archelaus, renowned philosophers and rulers, and Cato, a living embodiment of severity and austerity in Rome, used to alleviate their harsh and bitter cares of the soul with wine. May this remedy of wine please those who find it suitable. There are other remedies that appeal to me, perhaps not so different from these, but more fitting and appropriate for a moderate and steadfast individual. First of all, I admire the example of Achilles from Homer, who used to soothe his soul and find respite from his numerous military duties by singing along with the lyre, a musical instrument. Hence, I believe our Virgil introduced his Polyphemus in a cave, where "Fleecy sheep accompany him; his only pleasure and solace from sorrow hangs from his neck, a pipe." And certainly, in this matter, I agree with the opinion of the Pythagoreans, who affirmed that our soul gathers and composes itself in tranquillity and peace when soothed and comforted by the sweet voices and melodies of music. I have experienced this not infrequently in myself, as in times of mental fatigue, the sweetness and variety of sounds and singing have lifted me up and restored me greatly. You will experience this too, if it ever happens to you: no matter how burning your worry may be, it will immediately fade away if you persist in singing. And I don't know why it seems to me that my own singing, whatever it may be, satisfies me and benefits me more than the playing of any other excellent and highly skilled musician. Nor was that ancient custom, which was later prohibited by the Council of Aries, without merit. It was the custom of singing at funeral processions. I believe the ancient good people did this to distract their minds from the gloomy thoughts of death. But perhaps our most devout individuals found it more useful to remember that they, too, are mortal like the deceased. They considered it a more pious duty to acknowledge their mortality and their gradual decay with each passing hour, rather than engaging in any frivolity and indulgence. However, delving further into this discussion would be out of place. I affirm that whatever we do to entertain ourselves, as long as it is done without harm to others, is not unworthy of a studious person. Plutarch says: "Moving from place to place is like imitating someone in flight." And surely, it is beneficial to seek new amusements in various locations and enjoyments: running, jumping, throwing, whistling while hunting, and among young people, in a suitable place and time, I do not dislike it. Nor would I be displeased with socializing, bantering, spending the night with lights, playing with your friends and young people, and even singing while dancing. Our poet exclaimed: "I do not like this game; I shout and ask for a different one."

It wouldn't entirely displease me if some slightly lascivious games pleased those who needed to forget their mental distress. Lucius Sulla often sang, and Cimon, the renowned Athenian, sang after dinner with Laumedon. Scipio, who was not only a shining example of Roman military prowess but also a prominent figure of Latin civilization, used to dance with great grace. Even Appius Claudius, a man who triumphed and was mature in age, willingly and joyfully danced in his later years. Augustus, the first successor to Caesar, who thrice closed the Temple of Janus Quirinus, reportedly enjoyed fishing with a hook for his amusement and occasionally played marbles with several children who were sweet-looking and outspoken. Wasn't Heraclitus, the philosopher, seen playing knucklebones with children near the Temple of Diana? And Socrates, the paragon of modesty and seriousness, didn't he play similar childish games with children for recreation? Lelius and Scipio used to entertain themselves on the shore near Gaeta by playing with pebbles, making them skip on the water and marvellously rejuvenating themselves together. I will mention what comes to mind in relation to this similarity. Publius Mucius, a jurist, played the game known as "duodecim scripta" to relax, and Claudius Caesar played the game called "alea." He even wrote a book about it, not only to explain the strategies needed to win but also, perhaps, to derive pleasure from writing about it. Similarly, Gaius Matius and Marcus Ambivius, Roman patricians, wrote those two books "Quocum et Pistorem," where they command that when coming into contact with a woman, they should wash their hands in a river before touching anything. They wrote not to teach bread baking and cooking but, I believe, only to imitate Solon, the most distinguished ruler and philosopher in Greece, who, according to

Plutarch, used to indulge in writing lascivious verses to relax from the exertions of his duties.

In Homer's tale, Penelope, I believe, took delight in keeping twenty beautiful, blonde geese and enjoyed pampering them, perhaps to forget about her beloved Odysseus while she took care of her household and family. Alexander, the noble Roman prince who despised thieves, reputedly kept twenty thousand pairs of doves as pets and fed on the fruit of their crops. He took pleasure in watching them fly and, as the poets say, enjoyed hearing their coos of love and their winged applause for those who nurtured them well. The historian Suetonius recounts that the Roman emperor Tiberius found amusement in swimming amidst numerous young children in the bath, laughing and calling them his little fishes. Ulysses used to bathe with fragrant oils near Circe. Cato, the honourable Roman, would take a break from his duties and weave small baskets. I have witnessed some individuals who were rigid, eccentric, and unyielding, to the point where, to push out a broken nail, another whole nail had to be driven into it. To overcome their stubbornness, one had to engage in arguments and provoke them into a fight until they released their frustration. Afterward, they became gentle, easy going, and flexible in every way. According to the historian Diogenes Laërtius, the philosopher Pirro of Elis, son of Plistarchus, found amusement in keeping a clean and well-groomed sow, perhaps even holding it like a baby in his arms. There are many similar examples and methods to alleviate the burden of harsh thoughts and restore ourselves.

If I were to consider them, I could present them to you, as our ancestors used to find recreation in them. But for now, let these examples suffice for our purpose.

Therefore, when sad memories arise and turbulent thoughts and anxieties overwhelm us, and when heavy and burdensome worries start to oppress us, we must immediately resist them before our mind is convinced, for the mind can never regain control once it succumbs. At the first signs of such attacks, we should quickly employ similar remedies and diligently strive to restore our peace of mind and mental freedom. As the saying goes, if one remedy does not suffice, many may prove helpful. Therefore, we should try different methods until we find someone who can bring tranquility and peace to our own mind.

There are a few more excellent suggestions on this matter that I don't want to overlook. They are as follows: Do not dwell on past misfortunes; engage in conversations with yourself and others about anything other than your own troubles and misfortunes. In Rome, the statue of the goddess Angeronia had her mouth bound and sealed, and the priests offered sacrifices to her in the sanctuary of the goddess Voluppia. Macrobius interprets this mystery as signifying that by silently enduring the anguish of the soul, it eventually transforms into pleasure. However, because it seems that when we are alone, we cannot help but dwell on our own troubles, and when we are not alone, we find solace in the memories and admonitions of those who listen to us, I endorse the ancient precept that in times of unhappiness and misery, one should always avoid solitude. It is praised to be in the company of dear acquaintances and friends in theaters, during festivals, and private and public gatherings. Similarly, I praise the idea of retreating to the countryside with youth, enjoying the open air on those joyful hills, amidst beautiful gardens and pleasant meadows. And to divert your mind from every sad memory and harsh thought, I tell you this: you will find nothing more beneficial than engaging your body and occupying your mind with various tasks, whether they be pleasant or unpleasant.

So, when people saw Pompey lying dead and severed on the shore, they mourned him briefly before quickly fleeing. It would be beneficial to engage in activities involving birds, hunting dogs, trapping wild animals, or fishing. It is also helpful to take up the cause of a friend or neighbour and provide support in their legal case. By keeping ourselves busy with such exercises and avoiding idleness and solitude, we can achieve overall well-being.

I will not withhold my own experience on this matter. It may seem insignificant, but it offers an excellent and immediate remedy. Nothing contradicts my mental distress and brings me more peace and tranquillity than occupying my thoughts with a worthy task or engaging in challenging and rare investigations. I often memorize poems or excellent prose, analyse speeches, and expand arguments. Especially at night, when my mind is restless and awake due to my inner turmoil, I delve into unexplored ideas and mentally construct extraordinary inventions that move and accomplish great and invaluable things. Sometimes, not only do I find solace in these mental exercises, but I also come up with remarkable and memorable creations. In the absence of such investigations, I create complex structures in my mind, arranging columns with various capitals and bases, adorning them with unique frames and panels. I immerse myself in these activities until sleep takes over. And if these remedies do not suffice to restore my peace, I turn to understanding and discussing the hidden causes and workings of natural phenomena. Above all, nothing satisfies me more than mathematical investigations and demonstrations, particularly when I can apply them practically in life. Just as Battista drew principles for his painting from mathematics and derived incredible propositions concerning the movement of weights. I don't want to go into detail about how these mathematical arts affect me personally, nor do I want to dwell on convincing you of what I already mentioned earlier. I simply affirm this: nothing is more effective in dispelling sadness than engaging in other occupations and thoughts.

I confess that it has not been uncommon for me to find myself in the midst of envious, provocative, and troublesome individuals, who relentlessly provoked me with their words, trying to ignite my anger from every direction. However, I remained so engrossed in my own investigations and so determined to pay them no attention that they might as well have been the crow that greeted Caesar or the parrot that repeated its own name, for I neither heard, saw, nor felt anything other than myself. I engaged in introspection, revisited my studies and vigils, while promising myself good fortune and a lasting legacy. Consider, then, how filled my mind is with marvellous investigations.

Near Syracuse, during a great destruction of that noble city, Marcus Marcellus commanded his soldiers to spare the mathematician Archimedes. This remarkable man had defended his homeland by devising various war machines and previously unseen instruments, disrupting the enemy's plans and withstanding their assault. They found him working on geometric problems that he had drawn on the floor of his house, so absorbed and abstracted from all other senses that the noise of weapons, the cries of the wounded citizens, and the screams of the multitude overwhelmed by flames and the collapse of roofs and buildings did not disturb him. It is truly astonishing that such commotion, the thick smoke, and dust did not distract him from his mathematical investigation, to which he was so dedicated and absorbed.

So, do not doubt that if we establish within ourselves a good reason for living, engage in praiseworthy activities, persist in the pursuit of noble and outstanding endeavours, and embody virtue and steadfastness, we can certainly overcome adverse circumstances, wearisome hardships, pain, and all forms of adversity and injustice inflicted by time and fortune, as well as the malice and wickedness of deceitful and wicked individuals in life. By doing so, we can attain true peace, joyful tranquillity, and a worthy serenity of mind.

end

This English translation is based on the Italian edition of Opere volgari vol. 2 by Leon Battista Alberti, edited by Cecil Grayson, 1966. The original work is in the public domain mark 1.0 - Creative Commons License

This edition was edited and translated by:
Brendon Carlin
Maria Paez Gonzalez
Sofia De Luca (psyoart)
2022

cover design:
Brendon Carlin

ISBN 978-1-7391605-1-7

LIMBO PRESS

www.ingramcontent.com/pod-product-compliance
Lightning Source LLC
Chambersburg PA
CBHW071358080526
44587CB00017B/3120